To dear Jamie
"In Memoriam" of her
Christmas visit of 1897
& 1898 — Winifred

A CRITICAL STUDY OF IN MEMORIAM

A CRITICAL STUDY

OF

IN MEMORIAM

BY THE

REV. JOHN M. KING, M.A., D.D.

PRINCIPAL OF MANITOBA COLLEGE
WINNIPEG

HASKELL HOUSE PUBLISHERS LTD.
Publishers of Scarce Scholarly Books
NEW YORK, N. Y. 10012
1971

Framingham State College
Framingham, Massachusetts

First Published 1898

HASKELL HOUSE PUBLISHERS LTD.
Publishers of Scarce Scholarly Books
280 LAFAYETTE STREET
NEW YORK, N. Y. 10012

Library of Congress Catalog Card Number: 75-171230

Standard Book Number 8383-1332-9

Printed in the United States of America

DEDICATED
TO
THE MEMORY
OF
MY WIFE

PREFACE

THIS small work on In Memoriam had its origin in a course of Lectures delivered to ladies in Manitoba College in the winter and spring of the present year. The Lectures, the main contents of which are embraced in this volume, were prepared without any intention of publication. They are put in print at the request of many who heard them, and, though the perusal of a summary however full, is a very different thing from the hearing of a lecture, especially when, as in the present case, the subject is a poem, which in reading it the tones of the living voice can do so much to interpret, they may perhaps interest a wider circle, and help some of its numerous readers to a better understanding of the meaning and a deeper appreciation of the beauty of the remarkable work.

Though not primarily intended for any wider class than that composed of the ladies who listened to them, the Lectures were not written without a good deal of care and without a somewhat close study of much of the voluminous literature on the subject to which they refer. Frequent references will be found throughout the book to more than one of the expositors of the Poem. While the Author would gratefully acknowledge his indebtedness to almost all of these for valuable suggestions, he has exercised throughout an independent judgment, and has not shrunk from calling attention to what appears to him to be the misapprehensions and the forced interpretations of one and another.

One of the earliest commentators on the Poem, and one of the first to recognize its significance for religious thought, as well as its literary charm was the Rev. F. W. Robertson, and though his small volume on the subject consists of nothing more than a brief heading to the successive poems or cantos, it is singularly valuable, as shewing what that brilliant and gifted man understood to be the leading thought of each. It will be observed that in several instances these headings have been transferred to the present work. They will be recognized by the initials (F.W.R.) of the famous preacher. Dr. Gatty's little volume, entitled a Key to In Memoriam, is instructive and helpful : it is especially so, because of some annotations written by the Poet himself, which are incorporated in it. Under the title of Prolegomena to In Memoriam, Mr. Thomas Davidson gives a full analysis of the Poem and discusses at considerable length and with much vigor some of the philosophical and religious questions which it raises. The Trancendentalism of Kant is perhaps too largely in evidence throughout this work. It remains true, nevertheless, that it evinces both wide reading and mental acumen, and gives valuable aid to the understanding of the Poem.

The most elaborate treatment of In Memoriam which has come under the Author's eye is that by Professor Genung. Its merits are such that no one making a thorough study of the Poem can afford to overlook it, or fail to derive profit from its careful perusal. At the same time, it is difficult to avoid the conclusion that its value is greatly impaired by a theory as to the aim and scope of the Poem, which leads the writer to ascribe to it a kind of unity on the one hand and a regularly graduated progress on the other, such as the circumstances attending its composition, as related by the Poet himself, must have prevented it from acquiring. As a result, and by way of sustaining this theory which is rigidly applied throughout, we have presented to us purely arbitrary and artificial divisions, connections equally arbitrary and artificial, and forced interpretations not a few. This, we are aware, is a severe charge to bring against a book of such note, but examples will be forthcoming in the following pages to sustain it fully.

Among others, Mr. Joseph Jacobs gives a careful, appreciative and minute word-study of the Poem. A thoughtful, appreciative and liberal criticism of it, from a Roman Catholic point of view, is furnished by Brother Azarias in his "Phases of Thought and Criticism." It is difficult to speak too highly of the Analysis of In Memoriam and the discussion of its contents, especially on the moral and religious side, by

Edward Campbell Tainsh in his volume entitled "A Study of Tennyson's Works."

The most effective treatment of In Memoriam, simply as a poem, is probably that of Stopford Brooke. His criticism of its literary qualities is at once discriminating and appreciative. By the assistance of his keen and practised pen we are enabled in some measure to understand the secret of that charm which all must recognize as belonging to the matchless word-pictures with which the Poem abounds. Not much importance apparently is attached to the Poem by this writer, as a plea for immortality. From Henry Van Dyke and W. J. Dawson we have also valuable and discriminating estimates of In Memoriam from the same point of view, combining however with the literary considerations, those of a religious character as well.

The most satisfactory book on the whole, in the way of assisting the student to read In Memoriam intelligently, is probably the small volume of Mrs. Chapman. Her analysis of the separate poems is very generally just, and the contents are summarized, always in correct, and sometimes in felicitous and graceful terms.

It would be too much to expect that the present critical study of the Poem should be free from mistakes. No such claim is made on its behalf. The author would not wish it to be brought into comparison with some of the works which have been named. It has, however, proved helpful in its spoken form to not a few, and it is now given to the public in the hope that it may assist a still wider circle to understand and appreciate a poem which is more than ever engaging the attention of those who use the English tongue, and in which the genius of the Poet wrestles with problems of undying interest to the human family.

MANITOBA COLLEGE, WINNIPEG.
November 4, 1898.

INTRODUCTION

TENNYSON is probably the greatest Poet of the Victorian era; without doubt In Memoriam is his greatest poem; the poem "most weighted with thought, most varied in feeling" and most perfect in form.

The occasion of the Poem, as is well known, was the sudden, and, as we might reckon it, the premature death of Arthur Hallam, a son of the famous historian, and a young man, according to the testimony of all who knew him, of remarkable intellectual promise and of very lofty character. The two young men, Tennyson and Hallam, seem to have met for the first time in 1828, when both went up to Cambridge as students. The friendships of students are proverbially close and confiding. The friendship then formed between these two youths was one of quite exceptional intimacy even for students. Common tastes, common ideals of a lofty character, even common pursuits—both being poets—supplied its foundation, and explain its closeness. Besides, they had ample opportunities to become fully acquainted with each other. They pursued their studies together for a series of years at the same University. They joined in debate and song at the meetings of its Societies. They visited at one another's homes, in Somersby and London. They travelled together on the Continent. In addition, Hallam became engaged to the Poet's sister, Emily. As the result of all, a friendship grew up between the two, which, as has already been intimated, was one of quite ideal intimacy and tenderness. This friendship in its earthly form was broken by the sudden death of Hallam at the age of twenty-two, in the city of Vienna and on the 15th of September, 1833. So much for the occasion of the Poem.

The Poem itself, the In Memoriam, consists of a hundred and thirty-one Cantos or, to speak more properly, small separate poems, together with a Prologue and what is termed an Epithalamium or marriage song. Two of these poems, the thirty-ninth and the fifty-ninth, were not found in the earliest edition; they must have been written subsequently to its appearance. This, the first edition, was given to the public in 1850, almost seventeen years, therefore, after Hallam's death. The separate poems were written, as we are told, at different times and at different places during this long interval, and in accordance with the prevailing thought and feeling of the Poet at the time. We see from the recently published Memoir of Tennyson that these hundred and thirty-one poems were not the only ones which he wrote on his friend. There were still others which were not allowed to find a place in In Memoriam, apparently as not coming up to the high pitch of excellence which he had marked out for the shrine in which the memory of his friend was to be encased, or perhaps as not sufficiently distinguished in thought and tone from those already incorporated in it.

The separate poems, as has been said, were not written in the order in which they are printed. It is important to bear this fact in mind. In forgetfulness of it, some commentators have sought to impress on the Poem a kind of unity, which is largely fictitious. In the order in which they are now found, the earlier poems are predominantly plaintive; they are weighted with the sorrow of separation and loss. In those which immediately follow this earlier part—those constituting the central portion of In Memoriam—the grief is, in the main, more subdued; it is such as to leave the mind of the Poet free to deal with the great questions of evil, of immortality, of the state of the departed, on the supposition that they are still consciously existent—questions which have so deep an interest for us all, but especially for those who have been called to part with those dearest to them. I have said, the grief in this central portion is *in the main* more subdued. The qualification is not unneeded; for perhaps there is no single poem in the whole series in which expression is given to a more bitter and even rebellious sense of loss than in one of the lyrics, (lxxii.) found within this part. In the latter poems, while the sense of loss has not disappeared, it has not only ceased to be tumultuous and bitter, it has become sympathetic, it is less personal, it has become in a manner even catholic. Again the doubts which were fought in the earlier portion have been overcome, or at least have ceased to find expression; and the prevailing state of feeling reflected, so far from being one of sorrow, or at best one of sullen resignation, is calm, confident, even victorious. The striking characterization of the Poem by Stopford Brooke is thus fully justified. "It is a song of victory and life arising out of defeat and death; of peace which has forgotten doubt; of joy whose mother was sorrow, but who has turned his mother's heart into delight."

As to the character of the Poem, it is not a mere elegy, like the Lycidas of Milton or the Adonais of Shelley. It has indeed this in common with both of these, that it gives tuneful expression to the sense of loss and of separation in death, and to the virtues of the departed, but it differs from them in that it raises and deals with the whole question of the Hereafter. This is after all the most distinctive feature of In Memoriam. It is a great philosophical and religious poem ; one which beyond any other takes its color from the age in which it was written, reflecting its doubt, and at the same time giving intense and beautiful expression to its faith. One may speak of it in this respect as a series of meditations on death, on God, and on immortality. The value of the Poem in this point of view has been variously estimated. Some who admire its literary beauty have been disposed to speak rather depreciatingly of it as an attempt to throw light on the difficult problems of existence. Others again, and among these some of the highest and most cultured minds, have regarded it as a priceless contribution to the religious thought of England. Apart from this, however, the Poem contains some of the most exquisite pictures both of nature and of domestic life, to be found in our own, or indeed, in any language.

Altogether the attention which the Poem is more than ever receiving, at least on this Continent, seems to warrant the belief that it will continue, at least for many years to come, to thrill with its blending beauty and pathos, the minds of those who speak the English tongue.

IN MEMORIAM

The Prologue

The Prologue is dated 1849, the year preceding that in which In Memoriam was given to the world. It was thus composed subsequently to all or nearly all the Cantos or separate pieces which go to form the Poem as a whole. It is to be regarded as embodying the conclusions reached by the Poet, in his long and perplexing musings on human life and human destiny, under the guidance of sorrow and of love. As such it deserves attentive study.

The religious character of the Poem is already apparent in this prefatory piece; addressed as it is throughout to the Son of God, the Christ in whose person the human and the divine meet in mystic union. Christ is also recognized as the Creator of the universe and of man, the source of all satisfying light on the great and perplexing questions of human character and destiny. As such He is to be regarded with reverence—not to fear Him is to mock Him—and to be met with implicit surrender of will. As over against this blessed invisible but not impersonal Presence, the necessary and undeniable limitations of human knowledge are explicitly recognized, and therewith the consequent need of faith, if the whole supersensible world is not to vanish from human thought. The Poem ends properly and worthily in a prayer, three times repeated, for forgiveness for any excess of grief, or for any even misdirected love which may have found expression in his songs, "wild and wandering cries," as he terms them, "confusions of a wasted youth."

"Strong Son of God, immortal Love;"

It seems almost unnecessary to say that the reference in these words is to the personal Christ, the Christ of the Gospels; or it would have been unnecessary to say it, if more than one of the commentators on the Poem had not shewn the inclination to deny the fact, and to make, as one of them does, the sole reference to be "to that Unseen Love which is, as he (the Poet) trusts, at the heart of things, in which all things live and move and have their being, which is perfect power and perfect tenderness and perfect justice."[1] There is really nothing in this introductory poem to warrant such an interpretation of its opening words, while there is very much throughout it that is irreconcilable therewith. Besides, we know on the best of testimony[2] that the Poet was a firm believer in the Incarnation and, other considerations apart, it would seem most natural to interpret the phrase "Strong Son of God" in the light of this belief.

But while it is the "Son of God" who is invoked in the Prologue, He is invoked, as the the words which follow shew, as the embodiment in human form of Love, victorious, immortal Love. The use of the capital letter indeed is almost equivalent to the identification by the Poet

---

[1]. Mrs. Chapman; the expositor who gives on the whole the best analysis of In Memoriam.
[2]. In addition to statements in his Memoir, the Poet's words, as reported by Dr. Gatty, may be quoted:—"I am not very fond of creeds; it is enough for me that I know God Himself came down from Heaven in the form of man."

of immortal Love with the personal Christ; it does not justify, however, any expositor of the piece in finding the personality of the Saviour merged in an impersonal principle, "that pure affection which as human love of friend for friend had worked as an ennobling power within the Poet's soul."[1]

This "Son of God" within whose heart love dwells as in its shrine, or rather who is love, as God is love, we that have not seen his face, embrace by faith, and by faith alone,

"Believing, where we cannot prove,"

"prove," *i.e.*, in the logical sense. Faith in the personal, the living Christ, is not the last result of an argument or of a series of arguments, is not the conclusion of a syllogism; or the faith, or what men term faith, which is thus produced, is of little moral value.

"Thine," as their Creator, "are these orbs of light and shade;" the planets, with particular reference probably to the sun and the moon. The three lines which follow bring us face to face with the mystery which the death of Hallam in early manhood had raised for the Poet, and which is being ever raised anew for us all: Death, God's creature, destroying Life, God's work. The mystery is set before us in a line full of vivid realism,

" . . . and lo, thy foot
Is on the skull which thou hast made."

---

[1]. Genung. It would be unfair to say that this author eliminates all reference to the personal Christ from the Prologue, but he makes the reference in it to the principle of love far more prominent than to the Person, in whom love is embodied. The inversion of the clauses in his analysis of the Prologue, thus—"Immortal Love, the Strong Son of God, is divine"—is itself as unwarranted as it is misleading.

But death is not the final experience for man. Even the hope of immortality which he finds within his breast—"he thinks he was not made to die"—affords a presumption to the contrary; and if, despite this presumption, he is still left in some doubt in regard to his final destiny, there remains the justice of the Creator, of Him who has been invoked as immortal Love, as a final refuge;

"And thou hast made him, thou art just."

Pursuing his address to Him whom he had designated in the opening words, "Strong Son of God," the Poet goes on to say,

"Thou seemest human and divine,
The highest, holiest manhood thou."

It should be obvious that the direct reference in these lines is not to an impersonal emotion, love "viewed as the efficient cause of the universe," (Mrs. Chapman); "the Christ nature rather than the Christ name," (Genung), but to the personal Christ, in whom in virtue of the incarnation the divine and the human to all seeming are united, with love indeed as the constitutive principle of His mysterious personality. Accordingly, the "manhood" here is specifically that of Him who stands at the head of humanity, the one sinless and perfect man. When, therefore, Davidson says in this connection and as illustrative of these lines, "The love which He is, is at the same time our Lord above us, and our holiest manhood within," he is at once reading into the passage a truth which, however important, is not the truth it is meant to convey, and missing another truth still more important—the perfection of humanity in the man Christ Jesus—which it directly states.

Of the two lines which complete the stanza the one asserts a significant philosophical truth, the other an equally significant religious truth. The philosophical truth is thus expressed,

"Our wills are ours, we know not how,"

Will as distinguished from desire; "that thou art thou," to use the poet's own words, "With power on thine own act and on the world," the possession and exercise of this power by a dependent being, is a mystery; one, as it appears from his Memoir, with which Tennyson was much exercised. He is not alone in feeling and confessing the mystery, which is far from cleared up by making, as he does, free-will "apparently an act of self-limitation by the Infinite." Sir William Hamilton, among others, pronounced the fact of human freedom, of free-will to be at once undeniable and inexplicable. This is precisely the purport of the line above. The fact is admitted, "our wills are ours;" the comprehensibility of the fact by the reason, or, at least, its actual comprehension is denied. "We know not how." With this is linked the religious truth,

"Our wills are ours, to make them thine."

This is the momentous significance of that freedom, that power of intelligent self-determination which lies at the basis of human personality, that it makes possible and therefore dutiful the surrender of our wills to Him who is sovereign Lord.

"Our little systems," systems, *i.e.*, of moral and religious truth, elaborated with more or less learning and skill, "have their day," often a brief one ; they come *to pass;* they disappear to give place to others.

> "They are but broken lights of thee."

They are "of thee," so far as they possess any truth whatever. They derive from Him who is "the light which lighteth every man that cometh into the world;" but they are all of them incomplete; the whole of truth is not contained in any one of the number. "They are but broken lights of thee," "And thou, O Lord, art more than they." The system has yet to be framed which gives "the Son of God" in His entirety.

The three stanzas which follow are among the most important in the Prologue for the right understanding of In Memoriam in those numerous passages which refer to the question of the existence of God and of Immortality. It will be observed that the Poet expressly distinguishes in them two states or attitudes of mind, designated respectively faith and knowledge; reserving the latter for that apprehension which the mind has of external objects and their relations, through the senses. What we see, hear, touch; that we know. We do not believe in its existence; we know it. The sense of sight,—" For knowledge is of things we *see*,"—is selected from among the senses, perhaps as the largest inlet of such knowledge. Of the whole supersensible world, the world of real being of which the senses give us no intimation,

> "We have but faith, we cannot know."

This distinction is in strict accordance with the predominant philosophy of the age in which In Memoriam was written—a period during which the phenomenalism of the great German philosopher Kant, was coming to be a prevailing element in British thought. We are not required to discuss at this time the validity of the distinction which is here drawn between knowledge as coincident with the realm of experience, and faith as relating to that which transcends experience; in any case we must recognize it in order to understand the Poem before us. Some, those for example who hold that the soul has a direct intuition of spiritual truth, would scarcely agree with the inferior place which the Poet apparently assigns to faith, when he says, "We have *but* faith."

But while he limits the sphere of knowledge, he is as far as possible from depreciating its importance. To him all truth, the truths of science, no less than those of religion, are from God. It is of the mind's apprehension of the former that he says,

"And yet we trust it comes from thee,
A beam in darkness, let it grow."

The reference, indeed, might be to faith and its contents, but what follows shews this to be unlikely.

Of this knowledge which has for its exclusive object the facts of experience and their laws, he goes on to say,

"Let knowledge grow from more to more."

The words bear testimony to a feature which has been regarded as a striking characteristic of Tennyson, and one of the secrets of his influence on the thought of his age—his profound interest in the scientific discoveries of the day, in the ever-widening boundaries of human knowledge. But not less characteristic of the Poet is the sentiment which finds expression in the line following,

"But more of reverence in us dwell."

The one must keep pace in its advance with the other; "that mind," the seat of intellect, "and soul," the seat of emotion, of spiritual feeling, apt to become divided and discordant in an enquiring and critical age, "according well, may make one music as *before*," when knowledge was so much more limited; "one music as before, but *vaster*," necessarily so, in virtue of the new strains which are making themselves heard for the first time. The Poet's sense of the need and the value of reverence in connection with the pursuit of knowledge finds emphatic expression in the lines which follow. If not suggested by, they are at least in strict accord with the words of the Psalm, "The secret of the Lord is with them that fear him." "We are fools and slight," *i.e.*, frail; "We mock thee when we do not fear." Compare cxiv. "Help thy vain worlds," vain, *i.e.*, as ready to be puffed up and carried away by knowledge dissevered from piety, "to bear thy light," the light of ever-enlarging discoveries of truth; termed "thy light," as reflected from the world which is the expression of His thought who gave it being.

The Prologue closes in three stanzas which, as has been said, have "the true ring of devout piety."

> " Forgive what seemed my sin in me,
> What seemed my worth since I began."

The reference in the first line may well be to the excessive grief for Hallam's death to which he had given way, and in the second to the devotion with which he had cherished his memory and to the pains which he had taken to enshrine his excellences in his song. In moments of severe self-scrutiny, the latter equally with the former may have appeared as needing forgiveness. There may well have been the consciousness with the Poet, when his work was completed, of mingled motive in the tribute in many respects unrivalled, which he had paid to his friend ; how seldom is a feeling of this kind entirely wanting even in the most self-forgetting services which we render to one another ! and accordingly he invokes even for the work by which he had immortalized his friend the divine forgiveness.

> " Forgive . . . .
> What seemed my worth since I began,
> For merit lives from man to man,
> And not from man, O Lord, to thee."

Who is not reminded by the last line of the words of the Saviour, "Even so ye also, when ye shall have done all the things that are commanded you, say, we are unprofitable servants ; we have done that which it was our duty to do." Luke xvii. 10 ?

The lines which signalize the victory that his faith has reached, after its agonizing conflict with doubt, are found in the second last stanza of the

Prologue, and accompanied with what appears to be a slight tinge of Pantheistic thought.

> "I trust he lives in thee, and there
> I find him worthier to be loved."

It is a note of humility which makes itself heard in the last stanza,

> "Forgive these wild and wandering cries,
> Confusions of a wasted youth,
> Forgive them where they fail in truth
> And in thy wisdom make me wise."

The whole Prologue, of which these lines form the worthy close, is alike weighty in thought and admirable in tone. It is little less than the Poet's confession of faith; that to which he was accustomed to point those who interrogated him as to his belief. The regret is, therefore, all the stronger that so many should have sought either to reduce to a minimum its recognition of the personal historical Christ or to eliminate it altogether. The view which the recently published Memoir gives us of the real sentiments of the author, shews what injustice is done, alike to him as well as to the Christian faith, by such interpretations. However he may have shrunk from defining his faith in the terms ordinarily employed by Christian people, In Memoriam alone, and this Prologue especially, is evidence that he accepted and prized the fundamental Christian verity of the Incarnation—God manifest in the flesh.

There is undeniable force in the words of Tainsh, one of the most satisfactory interpreters of Tennyson. "By this inscription on the threshold, he who essays to enter, may learn that not less to Religion, than to Art and to Human Love is this temple dedicated."

IN MEMORIAM

I.

THE GAIN ATTENDANT ON LOSS, CONDITIONED HOWEVER THROUGH THE CHERISHING OF LOSS BY LOVE.

WHILE this poem stands first in the collection, it must almost certainly have been written subsequently to many of them. Grief has already passed into the reflective stage, and at this stage the Poet recognizes the possibility of rising to higher attainments through the loss which has desolated his life. The poet to whom he refers in the opening lines is Goethe, not Longfellow who founded a poem, which he termed "the ladder of St. Augustine," on that father's words:—"*De vitiis nostris scalam nobis facimus, si vitia ipsa calcamus*,"—containing these lines:

> "'Tis sorrow builds the shining ladder up,
> Whose golden rounds are our calamities,
> Whereon our feet firm planting, nearer God
> The spirit climbs and hath its eyes unsealed."

The "dead selves" of Tennyson, which may become "stepping stones" "to higher things" are certainly not vices, as with Augustine, nor even calamities only, as with Longfellow, but those possessions or acquirements, which have formed our life in whole or in part, and which are either taken from us or voluntarily renounced. The friendship in its earthly form of Hallam, his "bosom friend and half of life" may well be regarded as the dead self in the present instance. "In all these dead," Vinet says, speaking of loved ones withdrawn from life "we ourselves die; a part of our life and of our heart is buried in each of these tombs."

But how difficult to anticipate, to apprehend in advance, the gain the slow work of years which is to come through loss and sorrow! This difficulty is finely expressed in the lines:

> "But who shall so forecast the years
> And find in loss a gain to match?
> Or reach a hand thro' time to catch
> The far-off interest of tears?"

Another possibility presents itself to the mind of the Poet; this, viz., that the loss might come to be forgotten in the course of years, and the sorrow vanish in this way. That were a result to be still more dreaded, for it would mean the loss of love, that is, the deterioration of the nature. To ward it off, therefore,

> "Let love clasp grief lest both,"

not grief only, but love with it

> "be drowned,
> Let darkness keep her raven gloss,
> Ah sweeter to be drunk with loss,
> To dance with death, to beat the ground,"

i.e., to be frantic with grief,

> "Than that the victor hours,"

the hours in that case victorious,

> "Should scorn the long result of love,"

i.e., the result in the long run of the affection he had cherished for his friend,

> "And boast,
> 'Behold the man that loved and lost,
> But all he was is over worn,'"

The man indeed survives, but his love is gone; he survives only as a decayed and cast off garment. This alternative, it is to be feared, is the one more frequently realized. The best commentary on the passage, with which we are acquainted is supplied by the words of an author already quoted, Vinet—words which point out both how the dreaded alternative is reached and what of loss it implies. "The greater part of men cannot barter away their need of consolation, nothing supplies its place, nothing can be taken in exchange; to blunt the sting of grief, time is better than pride, for time wears out the soul, as well as all the rest. Life thus becomes less sorrowful, but it also becomes less serious, less noble."

<hr />

In the first eight poems or Cantos, the Poet is wholly absorbed in the thought of his loss. His sorrow, as yet untouched by hope, is nevertheless solaced by song. The problem at this point, so far as there is one, is, what shall he do with his sorrow, how shall he turn it to account.

II.

FIRST MOOD OF SORROW—THE YEW TREE IN ITS UNCHANGING GLOOM A FIT EMBLEM OF HIS STONY GRIEF AND, AS SUCH, CONGENIAL.

We have in this poem the first marked instance of personification, of which there are so many examples in In Memoriam. The object personified is the immemorial yew of the Churchyard, with its roots reaching down to the mouldering dead, its sombre hue unrelieved by any spring, unbrightened by any summer, the church clock striking in its shadow the hours which measure out "the little lives of men;" fit type of his own mind at the time in its unrelieved gloom, and in its clinging attachment to the departed. In addition there seems to be an allusion in the last stanza to the benumbing effect in the first place of a great bereavement; the sorrow which can relieve itself in tears often comes later.

> "And gazing on thee, sullen tree,
> Sick for thy stubborn hardihood;
> I seem to fail from out my blood,
> And grow incorporate into thee."

We have in this poem the first example, of which In Memoriam supplies so many illustrations, of Tennyson's sympathetic dealing with nature, now reading his own feelings into its varied scenes, and now finding expression for these feelings in its diversified moods. The yew tree is again introduced in Canto xxxix., but with a certain modification. It is there described as "kindled at the tips." It is not to be supposed that the Poet, whose observation of nature was so close and accurate, was ignorant of the fact, that the yew tree bore blossom and seed like other trees, but in his own words, quoted by Dr. Gatty, "Sorrow only saw the winter gloom of the foliage."

"*Branding* summer suns," *i.e.*, summer suns which leave their hot mark on other forms of plant life; an example of the unusual use or epithets, to which In Memoriam owes not a little of its force and beauty.

Sick for," *i.e.*, desirous of "thy stubborn hardihood."

III.

MISGIVINGS AS TO THE PROPRIETY OF CHERISHING SORROW, WHICH WITH LYING LIPS ROBS NATURE OF REALITY AND PURPOSE, AND CLOTHES IT IN HER OWN DARK AND CHEERLESS HUES.

Reflection begins and with reflection the question arises, is sorrow to be cherished or is it to be crushed? The sorrow is specifically that of bereavement. It is personified and addressed;

"O sorrow, cruel fellowship,"

for the time being he finds himself mated with it.

" O priestess in the vaults of death,"

The figure is changed. The mate has become a priestess, performing her sad but sacred rites in the vaults where death reigns.

" O sweet and bitter in a breath."

This characterization might be expected to refer to the utterances of sorrow in the two following stanzas, but it seems impossible to discover anything in these to which the epithet "sweet" could be applied. There may therefore have been no connection intended in this line with what follows. The force accordingly may be "sweet" as the offspring of love; "bitter" as the

CANTO III.

the accompaniment of loss. "What whispers from thy lying lip;" "lying," as suggesting a false and deceptive view of nature and of human life. Some have regarded the epithet as too harsh. It is again applied in the same connection in Canto xxxix. She whispers, "The stars ... blindly run;" *i.e.*, without intelligent purpose or end; or, if there be any such, it is hidden from human discernment.

> "A web is woven across the sky,
> From out waste places comes a cry,"

that is, of anguish. There is no spot, however desolate, in which the wail of suffering is not heard. "And murmurs from the dying sun;" "dying," the reference may be to the slow but steady burning out of the sun's fires, with its gloomy suggestions as to the future of our planet. Nature herself, the visible universe, she pictures as a mere phantom, a ghostly unreal thing,

> "With all the music in her tone
> A hollow echo of my own;"

another example of the way in which the Poet uses nature to interpret and reflect his own feeling;

> "A hollow form with empty hands."

holding out the hope of good, but having

really nothing to bestow; an altogether dismal picture, but it is that which sorrow, unrelieved by any ray of hope, draws. Such power does she possess, the Poet will say, to robe nature in her own gloom, and to empty the universe of any wise and beneficent purpose. The question arises in his mind,

> "And shall I take a thing so blind,
> Embrace her as my natural good;
> Or crush her like a vice of blood,"

i.e., some inherited or at least inherent evil tendency,

> "Upon the threshold of the mind?"

crush her, that is, by thought, by reason, and crush her "on the threshold of the mind,"—a striking and appropriate metaphor, the force of which is not to be overlooked. It is really equivalent to this: refuse it entrance into the mind, as not in any way worthy of rational entertainment.

The reader will notice how different, how almost opposite, the Poet's thought in regard to sorrow is here, from that which it was in i., where he seemed resolved to cherish grief. The contrast is even greater which meets us in lix. There is nothing that need awaken surprise in this. The poet's mind, as everyone knows, is not governed by logic; consistency, at least of the formal kind, is the last thing we are to expect from him. One of the charms of In Memoriam indeed is the expression which it gives to numerous and widely diversified states of mind, all of them true to nature in some of its moods.

Sorrow, the Poet has told us in this poem, is a treacherous guide, is sure to mislead us, is full of illusion, is blind. But, on the other hand, it is equally true, and this too we shall find told us in In Memoriam before it ends, that sorrow is wise or makes wise, that it dispels illusions, sees truths which are hidden from the cold intellect, has visions and of reality too, which seldom or never greet the tearless eye. " Without sorrow," one has said, " what should we know?"

IV.

PICTURE OF HIS STATE, WHEN AS JUST PASSING INTO SLEEP, WILL IS GONE, AND THE HEART ABANDONS ITSELF TO FEELINGS WHICH ARISE SPONTANEOUSLY.

This poem is not without its difficulty; it has in point of fact received different interpretations from the expositors of In Memoriam. The situation described seems to be this : night has come; the tired will gives up the effort to control thought. His "will is bondsman to the dark." It is for the time being in chains forged by the night. As a result, he sits "within a helmless bark." The mind, no longer under the control of the will, muses under the sway of the prevailing feeling. Consciousness still remains, and it is dominated by the vague sense of something lost, some prized pleasure gone. Few will have any difficulty — none who have known great sorrows — in understanding the experience described; the dim sense of some nameless trouble haunting the last waking moments of the night, and then again the first of the morning, if not also disturbing the intervening hours with frightful dreams, to which there seems to be a reference in the first two lines of the last stanza.

"Break," the Poet says under this oppressive feeling, still addressing his heart, though now in the language of metaphor,

> " Break, thou deep vase of chilling tears,
> That grief hath shaken into frost ! "

It is said that water may be kept liquid below the freezing point, if it is kept perpetually still, but if disturbed, it becomes ice at once, and in the suddenness of the expansion may break the containing vessel; and the claim has been made, that the language before us has reference to this singular scientific fact. The Poet's intimate acquaintance with science makes this claim probably true.

In any case what is meant by the invocation, "Break thou deep vase," etc., is, his desire that his pent-up feeling should find some outlet.

This musing, aimless grief, not unsuitable to the night with its tired faculties, may not be continued into the day.

> " With morning wakes the will and cries,
> Thou shalt not be the fool of loss."

V.

THE HEART SEEKS RELIEF BY EXPRESSING ITS SENSE OF LOSS IN VERSE.

As yet his sorrow is not accepted; the aim is simply to dull its stinging pain; and this the Poet finds he can accomplish by the effort to express it in rhythmic language, which, "like dull narcotics," numbs pain. He will persist, therefore, in "the sad mechanic exercise," although the feeling occasionally arises that his grief is too large or too sacred for adequate expression in human speech.

> " In words, like weeds, I'll wrap me o'er,
> Like coarsest clothes against the cold : "

the term "weeds" is probably used here in its earlier signification of dress or clothing, without any regard to the mourning character of the apparel ; though in its later signification, seen in the expression "a widow's weeds," it would be far from inappropriate in this connection. The epithet "coarsest," as here employed, would seem intended to express the Poet's sense of the disproportion between the word clothing and the inward feeling, the roughness and hardness of the one, the delicacy and tenderness of the other. No poet had ever less reason to complain of the inadequacy of human language to express differing emotions and delicate shades of the same emotion ; but dowered as he was with great depth and wide range of feeling, he may well have felt, that words even in his hands were but an imperfect instrument for the expression of inward sentiment. The effort to express his grief in rhythmic words soothed him. " But," he tells us,

> " That large grief which these enfold
> Is given in outline and no more."

It may be stated that by Genung, this and some other poems, to be cited as we advance, have been termed chorus poems, being distinguished from the great body of the work, as portraying the singer's mood, rather than giving formal expression to his thought.

VI.

No consolation in the thought that human life is full of similar tragic experiences.

The son perishes on the field of battle at the moment when the unwitting father is drinking his health; the sailor boy finds his watery grave as his mother's head is bowed in prayer on his behalf, and the lover meets his sudden death at the time when his love is decking herself for his reception, even as his friend Arthur had taken his departure from life at the very time when he himself was wistfully awaiting his return. There is no textual difficulty to be dealt with in this poem. The language is as simple and noble as the sentiment is deep and thrilling. What is required is, that the reader keep his nature open to the tender pathos by which it is pervaded and which appears to increase, till it finds a fitting climax in the words:

> "O what to her shall be the end?
> And what to me remains of good?
> To her perpetual maidenhood,
> And unto me no second friend."

The reader will notice the strong and at the same time alliterative line in the 4th stanza, "His heavy-shotted hammock shroud," also the felicitous use of the epithet "wandering," as applied to a grave in the sea.

"Her father's chimney glows," (8th stanza), referring to the open fire-place of England.

VII.

THE DESOLATE HEART LENDS ITS OWN DARK COLOUR TO OBJECTS ONCE BRIGHT AND JOY-INSPIRING.

The picture is one of the utter desolateness consequent on the sudden shock of bereavement, as yet unrelieved by the touch either of hope or of resignation. The house in which Arthur had lived is revisited in the grey of early morning. It is "dark house," the street on which it stands is "the long, unlovely street;" "Like a guilty thing," with a heart as burdened as that of one on whose conscience some great crime lies, with some such shrinking from the presence of his fellows as the criminal feels, he creeps " at earliest morning to the door."

> " Doors, where my heart was used to beat
> So quickly, waiting for a hand,
>
> A hand that can be clasped no more."

There is no mistaking the effectiveness and the beauty of these lines. The contrast of the *then* and the *now* could hardly be made more touching than by this detail:

> " . . . waiting for a hand,
> A hand that can be clasped no more."

In the concluding stanza, the Poet, as so often, finds his desolate mood reflected in nature with its " drizzling rain," while " far away the noise of life begins again." The rush and roar of business is resumed regardless of individual loss and sorrow. The last lines are peculiarly strong, and with their harsh sibilants, they seem as if charged with the gloom and the drizzle of the opening day ;

> " And ghastly through the drizzling rain
> On the bald street breaks the blank day."

The hard alliteration in the last line will not be overlooked.

VIII.

Scenes of former enjoyment, unattractive in the absence of the loved one—The fostered flower.

This is a companion picture to the former. In both, expression is given to the common, or rather, the universal experience of the fading of the light from familiar and cherished scenes, when the loved one is absent or has withdrawn; but in the latter poem the lonely heart is relieved by some memento of the vanished presence.

The Poet compares himself in his bereavement to the lover disappointed in finding " her gone and far from home " whom he had come to visit, and for whom " all the magic light," the light which acts like magic, light struck from the heart, " dies off at once from bower and hall." His is a precisely similar experience.

> " So find I every pleasant spot
>   In which we two were wont to meet,
>   The field, the chamber, and the street,
> For all is dark, where thou art not."

Yet as that lover's disappointment and grief are mitigated by some rain-beaten, wind-tossed flower on which his love had spent care, he, too, will find some solace for his stricken heart by planting on the grave of his friend the flower of poesy which was once his delight.. Poetry, it will be noticed, which was formerly the narcotic to dull pain, is now refreshing to his spirit, as the flower "which pleased a vanished eye." The author is not confident that it will live—this poem may have been written in the earlier years of the Poet's course, when his fame was far from assured—but even if it die, it shall die planted on the tomb of his friend.

The Cantos, or rather brief poems, ix.—xvii., are written, or are at least supposed to describe the Poet's feelings, during the course of the ship's voyage which brought the body of Arthur to England. ix. and x. are companion poems, in both of which the mind of the Poet is intent on the vessel with "its dark freight."

IX.

"Benison on the ship which brings back the remains of one 'more than a brother.'"
F.W.R.

The thoughtful reader will be conscious of a change in the tone of the Poem at this point. Hitherto it has been one recurring note of plaintive grief, or of desolate sorrow ; the tone now is one of tender and clinging love. This poem is remarkable at once for the depth of affection which it discloses, and for the manner in which the affection is portrayed. It is represented as passing over to the vessel, "the fair ship," which bears the "loved remains" " to those that mourn in vain ;" and which in language reflecting at every turn the rich fancy of the Poet, is invoked to bear them swiftly and peacefully under "gentle winds and through prosperous floods."

More than one expression in the piece deserves attention, as illustrating the richness of the Poet's fancy, and his felicitous use of words. "A favorable speed ruffle thy mirrored mast ;" the allusion being to the circumstance that the swifter the vessel's speed, the more would the reflection of the mast on the agitated waters be broken. "Thro' prosperous floods," *i.e.*, floods (of ocean) which prosper or speed the vessel in its course. "All night no ruder air perplex thy sliding keel ;"— the use of the metaphorical term "perplex," has striking force and beauty in this connection,—"Till Phosphor," the morning star, "through early light shall glimmer on the dewy decks." We are introduced in the last stanza to another striking metaphor, "my widowed race." The line is repeated in xvii. The skill of the Poet in the use of words, so that their very sound seems charged with the sentiment seeking expression, is very conspicuous in the fourth stanza:

> "Sphere all your lights around, above;
> Sleep, gentle heavens, before the prow;
> Sleep, gentle winds, as he sleeps now,
> My friend, the brother of my love."

X.

His friend's burial beside or within the quiet church more consonant to human feeling than his burial in the turbulent sea.

In imagination the Poet follows the vessel in its course, follows it day and night;

> "I hear the noise about thy keel;
> I hear the bell struck in the night;"

"the bell," that is, which was telling the hours on the ship; the poet's liking for the particular, his careful avoidance of the general, is well seen in this stanza, as in so many parts of In Memoriam. Then we have an effective use of contrast in the second stanza; in which, addressing the ship, he says:

> " Thou bring'st the sailor to his wife,
> And travell'd men from foreign lands;
> And letters unto trembling hands;
> And thy dark freight, a vanished life."

This peaceful transport which he sees in imagination, is pleasing to the "home-bred fancies," and so, though it makes really no difference, yet as the effect of association, and of habit, it seems sweeter,

> " To rest beneath the clover sod
> That takes the sunshine and the rains,"

that is, to be laid at rest in the open churchyard,

> " Or where the kneeling hamlet drains
> The chalice of the grapes of God ; "[1]

that is, within the church, and near the altar-rails where the wine of the sacrament is dispensed to the kneeling worshipper, than that "the roaring wells" of ocean should, together with the ship,

> " . . . gulph him fathom deep in brine;
> And hands so often clasped in mine,
> Should toss with tangle[2] and with shells."

The last two lines supply an example of very vivid realism. The poem, throughout, gives striking and effective expression to the instinctive feeling of at least all Christian people.

₁ "The fruit of the vine," Matt. 26: 29.

₂ "Tangle"; sea-weed, or "oar-wood, such as grows at the extreme tide limits, where its long fronds rise and dip in the water."—(ROLFE).

XI.

THE PROFOUND STILLNESS OF AN AUTUMN MORNING MIRRORS TO HIM AT ONCE THE CALM OF SPENT PASSION IN HIS OWN BREAST, AND THE CALM OF DEATH IN HIS FRIEND'S.

This poem is one specially deserving of study, not only because of the skill with which a few striking features in the landscape are selected, and of the beauty with which they are described, the marvellous adaptation of the language to the thought, so that the calm of which the poem speaks, seems to steal over us, as we read the words; but also because it supplies us with a typical example of the Poet's method of employing nature to reflect his own changing moods. This indeed is one of the secrets of the charm which In Memoriam has for the appreciative reader.

The landscape is not that of Somersby, the Poet's residence, but "some Lincolnshire wold, from which the whole range from the marsh to

›the sea was visible." It lies in the calm of autumn with its reddening leaf, the stillness so complete that it is broken only by the chestnut's pattering fall; and lying thus, in its wide and peaceful sweep, it both resembles the new feeling arising within him; the calm, not of submission indeed, but of spent tumultuous grief, and is distinguished from it, for his is a sullen and not yet a silver calm.

The effect of the poem is no doubt due in some measure to the frequent repetition of the epithet "calm," and the varied elements in nature,—air, earth and sea,—and in man, to which it is applied. "Calm and deep peace on this high wold," "Calm and still light on yon great plain," "Calm and deep peace in this wide air," "Calm on the seas and silver sleep," "And in my heart, if calm at all, if any calm, a calm despair." The last stanza is especially beautiful: "the silver sleep" on the sea, and "the waves that sway themselves to rest;"

> "And dead calm in that noble breast
> Which heaves but with the heaving deep."

"The bounding main"; the sea as forming in one direction the limit to his view.

"Lessening towers"; towers, that is, which seem to grow less as the distance at which they stand is increased.

"The silvery gossamers, that twinkle into green and gold;" a striking picture and one testifying to the Poet's minute observation of nature.

CANTO XII. 33

XII.

A STATE OF ECSTASY, DURING WHICH THE SPIRIT OF THE POET, ABSENT FROM THE BODY, WINGS ITSELF TO AND LINGERS BY THE RETURNING SHIP.

The calm of the preceding poem does not last; the calm of despair seldom or never does: the spirit of unrest returns. The carrier-pigeon with its message of woe attached to it, supplies the figure here, though there is an obvious reference also to the dove of Noah's ark (Gen. viii. : 8, 11), "Like her I go," "I leave this mortal ark behind." Compare "Our earthly house of this tabernacle," 2 Cor. v. : 1.

"A weight of nerves without a mind."

Such is his description of himself in his disembodied state, that state of trance or ecstasy, into which he represented himself as having passed; a bundle of sensibility without any controlling intelligence;

"And leave the cliffs,"

the white cliffs, by which the southern seas of England are bounded

" . . . and haste away
O'er ocean mirrors rounded large,"

with obvious reference to the rounded form and mirror-like face of the ocean, which his spirit traverses, until the sails of the vessel come in sight. Then the piteous cry arises,

> " . . . Comes he thus, my friend?
> Is this the end of all my care?"

The approach of the ship with the body of his friend, so eagerly desired, how little after all it is found to yield! "Is this the end?" Yesterday, a friendship so rich, so ennobling, so full of promise; to-day, faith apart, all that is left, a "breast, which heaves but with the heaving deep." "Is this the end? Is this the end?" It is the cry of keen and bitter disappointment; so little can that, which he meets on his dove-like flight, do, to rekindle the extinct flame of joy or even to mitigate the sense of loss. The last stanza describes the close of the trance. The spirit, after circling in the air, and playing about the prow of the vessel, returns " to where the body" that is, the body which it had left, his own body, "sits," and learns that he has "been an hour away."

It is difficult to know what exactly is to be understood in regard to a poem like this. The Poet, we are told, had a quite singular and marvellous power of passing into a state of insensibility to all external things, one approaching if not actually reaching that state of ecstasy, which we are accustomed to connect with the prophetic afflatus. Whether the poem describes an actual experience in the Poet's life, or is simply an imaginative picture of what might have been such, it is impossible to say. The truth in it remains in either case this ; that the sense of irretrievable loss is only deepened by the sight in fancy of the vessel, with its "dark freight, a vanished life."

XIII.

His loss seems unreal; it must be a dream —Time invoked to teach its reality.

At this stage reflection begins to work. Examining his consciousness, he finds a strange sense of unreality attaching to that which has transpired ; a common experience, especially when the bereavement has been sudden, and as yet is known only by report. Like the widower's tears, which mourn the "late-lost form" revealed in sleep, but not restored to his doubtful arms, so his, too, who weeps " a loss for ever new," a void which nought can fill, a silence never to be broken here.

The third stanza is a very striking one, and is

perhaps meant to explain, not only the greatness of the loss he mourns, but the sense of unrealness regarding it which he feels. Death is so unlike every other human experience. It puts an absolute close to our connection with him who has undergone it. And it is the disappearance, not of "a breathing voice," but of "a spirit;" the quenching, as it might seem, of a spark struck from Deity itself. No wonder the Poet terms it :

> "An awful thought, a life removed,
> The human-hearted man I loved,
> A spirit, not a breathing voice."

Difficult as he feels it to be to realise the death of this "more than brother," he invokes time to teach him "many years," *i.e.*, for years to come —as if a lesson which could not be learned in a day—that he does not suffer in a dream, but that "the comrade" of his "choice" has for ever gone from earth.

XIV.

THE SAME SENSE OF UNREALITY ATTACHING TO HIS FRIEND'S DEATH.

This is obviously a companion poem to the last ; only the failure to realise the fact of

Arthur's death is still more striking here; so complete is it indeed, that, standing "muffled round with woe"—a very strong expression—on the wharf which the ship touches, were his friend to step "lightly down the plank" with the other passengers, with "no hint of death in all his frame," he "should not feel it to be strange." This no doubt depicts an actual mood, in which the Poet found himself once, or it may have been more than once. The details are wrought out with equal simplicity and beauty, and the whole picture is a wonderfully vivid one.

The same difficulty in realising the death of one dear, finds touching expression in Cowper's poem on the death of his mother, and in Wordsworth's "We are Seven."

XV.

THE UNREST OF HIS TUMULTUOUS FEELING FINDS NOT ONLY ASSUAGEMENT IN NATURE'S CALM BUT SOMETHING CONGENIAL EVEN IN ITS STORM.

The poet, like all highly sensitive spirits, loves to have nature in sympathy with his changing moods. We have had one striking example of this in our Poet's case in x. There it was nature's morning calm that reflected his mood ; here it is her wild tumult, as the day declines to night. The picture of the storm in this poem is one of the Poet's master-pieces ; each effect in the sky, on the water, and on the land is wrought out in little more than a single word ;

> " The rooks are blown about the skies ; "

a line of great force, vividly picturing the fury of the gale, and filling with it the whole heavens.

> " The forest crack'd, the waters curl'd,
>   The cattle huddled on the lea,
>   And wildly dash'd on tower and tree,
> The sunbeam strikes along the world."

The intensity of the storm and its wild, wide sweep are thus presented to us in words, almost each one of which forms a picture ; especially striking, as shewing a close observer, as well as a powerful delineator of nature, is the view of " the low shaft of storm-shaken sunlight dashed " across the landscape.

On this tempestuous night the ship with the body of Arthur on board is on its homeward passage. In his fancy, he sees it gliding gently over a calm sea, "athwart a plane of molten glass ; " but for this fancy, assuring him of the safety of the vessel with its sacred freight, he could scarcely endure the strain of the surrounding storm. And yet on the other hand, but for the fear that the fancy is a mistaken one and that it is not thus "calm on southern seas,"

> "The wild unrest that lives in woe
> Would dote and pore on yonder cloud."

"cloud," which bears the rising wrath of the storm in its breast, as on something entirely congenial—the "cloud"

> "That rises upward always higher,
> And onward drags a laboring breast,
> And topples round the dreary west,
> A looming bastion fringed with fire."

This last stanza is peculiarly powerful. The agony of the storm is almost audible in the words "And onward drags a laboring breast;" its glory is finely pictured in the same cloud, which as the sun is setting becomes "a looming bastion fringed with fire."

"The cattle huddled" (2nd stanza), crowded confusedly together.

XVI.

The changing moods of which he has been conscious become an object of enquiry to him.

This poem is at once introspective and metaphysical. His sorrow has been now "calm despair," now "wild unrest." What do these changes mean? Is sorrow, which is his abiding feeling, itself susceptible of this alternation between extremes so wide apart, or, knowing "no more of transient form," that is, having no more inherent form even of the passing kind, than the dead lake which simply reflects on its surface what hangs above it, "doth she only seem to take the touch of change in calm or storm," or, a third alternative, has the shock of grief unhinged his reason, so that he is no longer able to distinguish, to keep apart—the work of intelligence—blending views and feelings, but unconsciously "fuses old and new," past and present, and made him,

> "that delirious man
> Whose fancy fuses old and new,
> And flashes into false and true,
> And mingles all without a plan?"

The dependence at times of our ideas and feelings on the aspects of nature around us, the degree in which these are frequently controlled and colored by these aspects is vividly pictured in the lake whose surface

> "holds the shadow of a lark
> Hung in the shadow of a heaven."

The comparison of the mind, under the sudden shock of grief, to the boat, which, striking against the shelving rock, "staggers blindly ere she sinks," and the metaphor "confused," as applied to the boat in these circumstances, deserve attention.

"Stunned me from any power to think," (4th stanza); an example of the condensed mode of expression, in which Tennyson so often indulges and which occasionally gives rise to obscurity.

"Fancy *fuses* old and new," (5th stanza). The metaphor, taken from the treatment of ore, is both obvious and striking.

XVII.

THE SHIP HAILED AND TENDERLY AND REVERENTLY BLESSED.

There is little which needs elucidation or remark in this poem. In it the affection entertained for Arthur is transferred to the ship which is bearing his remains to England, and the wish is expressed that all tempests which sweep the ocean may spare her, and all good influences attend her for ever. Attention may be called to a few of the expressions: "such a breeze compelled thy canvas," that is, impelled it. His own prayer is regarded with a fine play of fancy, as "the whisper of an air" to bear the vessel onwards "over lonely seas." The Mediterranean and the English Channel are far from "lonely," being, in fact, much frequented waters, but the Poet reads into them his own feeling. The burden which is borne across them, the loved companion silent in death, makes them "lonely" to him.

> "I in spirit saw thee move,
> Thro' circles of the bounding sky."

Such a circle, one which *bounds* the view for the time, is just that part of space included within the horizon. The "circles" or tracts of space would of course differ from day to day, as the vessel moved forward in its course, "My blessing *like a line of light* is on the waters," that is, such a stream of light on its forward course, as would enable it to avoid any danger. "And balmy drops," gentle and soothing influences, (compare "tired nature's sweet restorer, balmy sleep,") "in summer dark, slide from the bosom of the stars;" the stars, being viewed as in some way affecting the fates of men. Compare "ill-starr'd."

XVIII.

"The quiet english grave;" contending emotions of thankful acquiescence and of yearning desire.

This poem and the one which follows connect themselves with the place of burial. It is a consolation to him that the ashes of his friend are to blend with English earth, and rest "in the places of his youth." In this the Poet again expresses the instinctive feelings of the race. "'Tis well, 'tis something," "'tis little"; such are the terms in which his qualified satisfaction finds expression. Then in words of equal simplicity and beauty,—words, too, in which he surely interprets the better feelings of all, and has become the teacher of many,—he points out the character of those who may fittingly take part in the burial of the noble and loved dead

> "Come then, pure hands, and bear the head
> That sleeps, or wears the mask of sleep,
> And come, whatever loves to weep
> And hear the ritual of the dead."

And yet the yearning desire for the restoration

of the object of his affection makes itself felt within his breast. It finds expression in words suggested by the incident of the prophet and the Shunammite woman's child, 2 Kings iv. : 34.

> "Ah yet, e'en yet, if this might be,
> I, falling on his faithful heart,
> Would, breathing thro' his lips, impart
> The life that almost dies in me;
>
> That dies not but endures with pain
> And slowly forms the firmer mind."

These two last lines are particularly strong; it is difficult not to recognise in them as in so many other instances, the Poet's felicitous adaptation of the words to the thought.

XIX.

The poet finds a resemblance in the stream beside which Arthur was buried, to his own silence alternating with song.

Dying at Vienna on the Danube, the body of Arthur was brought to Clevedon in Somersetshire, and buried there at a point near where the Wye falls into the Severn. The Wye, like the Severn, is a tidal river, and thus, when the tide is full, the stream is hushed; when the tide ebbs, its purling voice is heard within its wooded banks, termed in the poem "wooded walls." Even so the Poet's grief for his friend's loss is sometimes too full for utterance; *then* he brims "with sorrow drowning song." After a season, a mood comes which permits utterance.

> "My deeper anguish also falls,
> And I can speak a little then."

At this stage in In Memoriam and for several Cantos onwards, the sorrow, it has been observed, is purely personal. It is instinct with the tenderness of youth, rather than with the thoughtfulness of maturer years, such as we are to see it become farther on. But in giving it expression, with what skill and delicate beauty the Poet weaves together the workings of nature without, and the alternations of feeling within!

XX.

THE GARRULOUS SPEECH OF THE SERVANTS, AND THE DUMB AND SCARED SILENCE OF THE CHILDREN IN THE HOUSE OF DEATH, SUPPLY HIM WITH ANOTHER ILLUSTRATION OF HIS OWN CHANGING MOODS.

There are griefs, "the lesser" ones, which may be spoken; they are relieved by words. They are not necessarily insincere, but they are not the deepest which we experience in seasons of bereavement.

> " There are other griefs within,
> And tears which at their fountain freeze."

The former resemble the grief of the servants in the house, where the now dead master lies, who " weep the fulness from the mind." His

> "lighter words are like to these,
> That out of words a comfort win;"

The latter resemble the grief of the children, who sit cold and silent in "that atmosphere of death." Everyone must recognize the aptness and the force of the comparison. How vivid, too, and how true to nature, the picture which the Poet draws of the blending grief and terror of the children!

> " For by the hearth the children sit
> Cold in that atmosphere of death,
> And scarce endure to draw the breath,
> Or like to noiseless phantoms flit."

XXI.

THE POET JUSTIFIES HIS PLAINTIVE SONG—SORROW HAS ITS RIGHTS; SORROW ESPECIALLY FOR ONE SO NOBLE, AND MUST NOT BE DENIED EXPRESSION.

This is regarded by Genung as another of the chorus poems, similar to viii. It opens as if Arthur's grave had been in the churchyard, and not in the chancel of the church, as it actually was. The explanation may either be, that the Poet was ignorant at the time of its composition of the exact spot of burial, or that this is an instance of poetic license. His song, so plaintive, so full of personal sorrow, is viewed as open to the charge of weakness, of affectation, of indifference to public interests of overwhelming moment, and to the advancing march of science, so remarkable at the time. It is justified, nevertheless, by the distinguished worth, unequalled among his compeers, of him whom it mourns,

"Ye never knew the sacred dust,"[1]

and by its instinctive character; his song is the natural, spontaneous, even irrepressible outburst of the emotion within. Nature supplies him with an instance of the like necessity; the gay note of the linnet, when the young she has bred take wing ; the plaintive note of another whose brood has been stolen.

> " I do but sing because I must
> And pipe but as the linnets sing :
>
> And one is glad; her note is gay,
> For now her little ones have ranged ;
> And one is sad ; her note is changed,
> Because her brood is stolen away."[2]

---

[1] The most striking testimonies are borne alike to Hallam's intellectual endowments and his moral excellence by the greatest of his cotemporaries. Alford says of him : "He was a man of wonderful mind and knowledge on all subjects, hardly credible at his age. I long ago set him down for the most wonderful person I ever knew. He was of the most tender, affectionate disposition." Gladstone, himself the greatest Englishman of his day, says: "When much time has elapsed, when most bereavements will be forgotten, he will still be remembered and his place, I fear, will be felt to be still vacant." Almost the last, if not the very last production of this distinguished man, was a tribute in one of the Reviews to the greatness and the worth of him whom he had parted with more than sixty years before.

[2] The last stanza affords an example of the alterations, and in this instance, at least, the improvement which the poet made on the earliest form of the poem. The lines originally read :

> "And unto one her note is gay,
> For now her little ones have ranged;
> And unto one her note is changed,
> Because her brood is stolen away."

XXII.

The brief but joyous companionship interrupted by death.

The Poet at this point reverts to the past, which he reviews in this and the three following poems. In the one before us, he sings of that sweet fellowship, "full of hope and song," which had brightened life to him for four happy years. "The path by which we twain," —the old poetic word,—"did go,"

"Thro' four sweet years arose and fell,"

summer being regarded as the zenith to which the year rises from the depths of winter, to descend again to winter through autumn's slope. The fifth autumn their fellowship is broken, as "following hope," they encounter "the Shadow feared of man." The expression, "following hope," is designed no doubt to convey the idea that their path was one not only full of present gladness, but also lighted up by anticipations of still brighter joys, as that of youthful companionship so commonly is. This unwelcome presence changes all; the lot of the Poet as well as and only in a less degree than that of his friend. The two last stanzas which describe the change are among the most vivid and original in the whole Poem.

> "Who broke our fair companionship,
> And spread his mantle dark and cold,
> And wrapped thee formless in the fold."

"Formless in the fold;" the alliteration, of which the Poet makes so frequent use in In Memoriam, will be noticed. The reference can scarcely be to the cerements of the tomb, in that case there would be a very unnatural sequence in the line which follows :

> "And dull'd the murmur on thy lip."

The absoluteness of the separation effected in death has nowhere found more touching expression than in the closing lines of the poem :

> "And bore thee, where I could not see
> Nor follow, tho' I walk in haste,
> And think, that somewhere in the waste
> The Shadow sits and waits for me."

XXIII.

Contrast of the past and the present.

The glad past is still vividly before him. The Poem is here also true to nature. Never does the mind revert so often to the past, or dwell on it with such fondness, as when some great bereavement has changed all of life. That past he contemplates, sometimes in silence, as shut within his sorrow, sometimes "breaking into song." With it present to his mind, he wanders in solitary thought to where the Shadow sits. In other words he places himself in imagination in the presence of death, and thence looks both back to the past and forwards to the future. "The Shadow fear'd of man" is now

> "The Shadow cloak'd from head to foot,
> Who keeps the keys of all the creeds."

The metaphor in these lines has been very freely criticised, but even those who have characterized it as halting or incongruous, have been constrained to admit its originality and its power. The reference in the latter line, which has passed as a permanent element into British thought, is to the fact, that it belongs to death, and to death alone, to clear up the mysteries relating to God and immortality. It has the prerogative to say the final word as to what is true, and what is not in the various creeds. In his reverie, he has but one feeling, "How changed" all!

The poem closes with a charming picture of the pure and lofty pleasures, which had marked and blessed the companionship so suddenly interrupted. Among these are recounted, the enjoyment together of the lavish beauty of nature, the swift play of gleaming fancy, and of rapid thought, ennobling converse with the philosophers and the poets of the olden time; all together enriching and enlivening life to such a degree that as memory recalls the past he can only say:

" And all we met was fair and good,
   And all was good, that time could bring,
   And all the secret of the Spring
Moved in the chambers of the blood."

"Breaking into song *by fits*" (1st stanza). We now know from the Poet's memoir, that In Memoriam was written through a course of years, at various times and places, where the author happened to be, in Lincolnshire, London, Essex, Gloucestershire, Wales, anywhere as the spirit moved him.

"**Often falling lame**" (2nd stanza). With reference doubtless to the difficulties regarding God and the Hereafter which arose in his own mind in the earlier stages of his grief.

"**And fancy light** from fancy caught" (4th stanza), *i.e.* The imagination of the one was kindled by, caught light from, the imagination of the other.

"**The secret of the spring**" (5th stanza). The expression is both an original and a suggestive one, embodying the mysterious reviving life of tree and flower. The conception of this moving "in the chambers of the blood" is certainly a bold one.

XXIV.

THE GREATNESS OF THE CONTRAST WHICH IS FELT BETWEEN THE PRESENT AND THE PAST RAISES THE QUESTION WHETHER THE PAST WAS REALLY SO COMPLETELY HAPPY AS IT NOW APPEARS.

This poem consists in a series of interrogations, very natural in the circumstances. Was his happiness in the companionship of his friend so perfect after all? Even the sun has its dark spots;

> " The very source and fount of day
> Is dash'd with wandering isles of night."

surely a very felicitous characterization of these spots. If it were thus perfect, earth had remained the Paradise, it has never been since, (in the earliest edition of In Memoriam), " Adam left his garden yet," (in later editions) " since our first sun arose and set." The change is a great improvement, so far as the poetry is concerned, but not as regards the truth expressed. The words as they now stand, exactly construed, really involve the denial of the existence of any primitive Paradise whatever. Or, having in view the well-known powers of a dense mist to magnify, as well as sometimes to distort objects beheld through it, is what appears the greatness of his former happiness due to "the haze of grief" through which he comtemplates it? Or again, is it simply an example of the effect of contrast in heightening impression?

> "The lowness of the present state
> That sets the past in this relief?"

Or finally, is it an instance of the familiar experience of "distance lending enchantment to the view?"

> "Or that the past will always win
> A glory from its being far;
> And orb into the perfect star
> We saw not, when we moved therein?"

In explanation of the last two lines, Dr. Gatty remarks: "We are told that if we were placed in the moon we should see the earth as a 'perfect star,' having a shining surface, and being thirteen times larger than the moon itself." Genung's explanation is in these words: "So perfect because the distant view changes it from nebular to orbic form." Both explanations of the Poet's language seem a little far fetched.

XXV.

LIFE'S BURDENS SHARED BY LOVE MAKE IT TO BE LIFE INDEED.

Having given tuneful expression in xx.—xxiv. to the happiness enjoyed in the companionship of his friend and to the sense of loss by which it has been followed, the Poet in this and the two following poems lifts Love into view as that which lends value to life, and that in the absence of which, life is to him not worth living. The keynote is thus struck of what one must regard as the central teaching of the Poem.

The questions of the preceding poem are not answered in this one; only the reality and the intensity of his former happiness is reasserted. Life had its daily burden then, as still, with him as with all. But in this burden lay the very condition of its gladness. It thus "needed help of Love," and Love was there by his side to give the help, to share the weight. "I know," says the Poet, with an unmistakable emphasis on the word, "I may not be able to answer my own questions, but I cannot be wrong in this,

"I know that this was Life."

This may mean either of two things : either that this sharing of life's burden by Love was the marked characteristic of the life which he had led during these four happy years, that which lay at its heart and was its principle, or, that this it was which lent existence its charm, made it Life indeed. The more obvious force of the words and the capital letter employed would seem to favor the latter as the meaning designed by the Poet ; the lines which immediately follow, however, agree better with the former rendering.

The poem takes a somewhat unexpected turn, and one not easily accounted for in the closing stanza :

> "Nor could I weary, heart or limb,
>   When mighty Love would cleave in twain
>   The lading of a single pain,
> And part it, giving half to him."

We are led to ask, is it not rather the part of love, to halve the burden of another and take it on itself, than to impose half its own burden on that other? No doubt the latter, too, displays the confidence of reciprocated affection. The characterization, moreover, of love as "mighty," being in the case before us, his own love, can hardly be regarded as felicitous.

As illustrating and confirming the sentiment of this poem, the words of Bacon may be quoted: " But one thing is most admirable, which is, that this communicating of a man's self to his friend, works two contrarie effects ; for it redoubleth joys and cutteth griefs in halves. For there is no man, that imparteth his joys to his friend, but he joyeth the more, and no man imparteth his griefs to his friend, but he grieveth the less."

"The track whereon with equal feet we fared" (1st stanza). We have in this line a good example of Tennyson's happy use of words in senses now rare. "Fared" is used in the old meaning of travelled (German *fahren*). The phrase "equal feet" is also a felicitous one— "feet" that is, keeping step with each other.

XXVI.

BETTER DEATH ITSELF THAN EXTINGUISHED LOVE.

That time can prevail over love, can eat the heart out of the affection which has given not happiness only, but nobleness to life, he longs to prove false, whatever "fickle tongues"—or the tongues of those who have fickle hearts—may say. The result is a possible one indeed, and, if there is any danger of its being realised in his case; still more, if the eye to which the future stands revealed,

> " That eye which watches guilt
> And goodness, and hath power to see
> Within the green the moulder'd tree,
> And towers fall'n as soon as built,"

if He,—whose prescience is such that He sees, even while the tree is green and flourishing, the internal decay which is sure to set in, and sees even while the tower is being built, its ultimate fall into ruins,—foresees his (the Poet's) love changed into indifference; then welcome death; life shorn of that which made it noble, is true life no more.

> Then might I find, ere yet the morn
> Breaks hither over Indian seas,
> That Shadow waiting with the keys,
> To shroud me from my proper scorn."

The two lines which close the third stanza supply a striking example of the condensed force of expression for which Tennyson is famous;

> " In more of life, true life no more;
> And love the indifference to be."

This poem marks, it will be noticed, a distinct stage in advance in the development of the

Poem ; lifting the reader up into a high plane, a plane far above that in which there is simply the bewailing, in however pathetic terms, of personal loss, and putting the crown on love, constant even in death, as that which gives true dignity to life.

"In Him is no before" (3rd stanza); in accordance with the philosophic conception that our time-determinations have no application to God. He is, *unzeitlich*, as the Germans have it.

"The morn" breaking over Indian seas, (4th stanza), is the Poet's way of saying "dawning from the east."

"My proper scorn," (4th stanza), is obviously, scorn of myself.

XXVII.

LOVE EVEN ISSUING IN THE PAIN OF LOSS IS BLESSED.

This is a kind of companion poem to the preceding, similar to that which we had in viii., as following vii. The theme is essentially the same, the inherent nobleness of love. To have loved, to have known the unselfish satisfactions which are experienced in the exercise of love, even though followed by the keen anguish of loss, is better than to have the immunity from trouble, which those enjoy who have never known what it was to love, and who had therefore nothing to lose. Love, the Poet has learned—and this may be regarded as the achievement of the introductory part of In Memoriam—is valuable not only for what it brings, fellowship, inspiration, mutual help; it is most of all valuable for what it is; and that abides or may abide, a treasure even when its object is removed. He does not envy, therefore,

"The captive void of noble rage,"

the lion which has lost its love of freedom and is content to be caged and fed, nor the linnet

"That never knew the summer woods,"

that has never tasted the sweets of liberty, nor the brute, devoid of conscience, indulging its propensities without restraint, and, just as little, the "rest" in man, the freedom from pain, which is begotten of want, that is, which is due to the absence of the nobler yearnings of the human soul, seen in "the heart that never plighted troth."

"I hold it true, whate'er befall,
I feel it when I sorrow most,
'Tis better to have loved and lost
Than never to have loved at all."

The words have gone into the English tongue, and are not likely to disappear from it soon.

What they express, however, it should be noticed, is not the indestructibility of true love —its survival spite of death and separation, that achievement is reached and signalized at a later stage in the Poem; it is simply the enrichment which comes to the life from having loved.

It seems difficult not to recognize that with the close of this poem a point of transition in In Memoriam is reached. One series of poems closes here; another series commences with the poem which immediately follows.

XXVIII.

Grief assuaged at the sound of the Christmas bells.

Up to this point the poem has been one long monody of grief, relieved mainly by the sense of the nobleness of the affection out of which the grief flows. At this stage the Poet's mind begins to deal, first, indeed in a direct manner in xxx., with the person of him, "his more than brother," who has gone from him in death. In doing so, the Poet enters the realm of faith, of revealed truth, indeed, and hence the propriety—not to be overlooked—of his entrance

into this new realm being synchronous with the observance of that festival, which commemorates the Incarnation, the birth of Him "who hath abolished death and brought life and immortality to light."

It is Christmas eve at Somersby, the first (one might almost think from the fourth stanza the second) since Arthur's death. The season, from its very nature and associations, both revives the sorrow and touches it with joy;

> "Four voices of four hamlets round,
>   From far and near, on mead and moor,
>   Swell out and fail, as if a door
> Were shut between me and the sound."

These, the blending bells of four village churches, are not to be identified. It is possible that they existed only in the fancy of the poet. They proclaim

> "Peace and good will, good will and peace,
>   Peace and good will to all mankind."

The rhythm in these lines seems an imitation, in a way, of the chime of bells. There is something, one can hardly help feeling, of overstrained sentiment in the fourth stanza. "This year I slept and woke with pain," etc., to which one is not reconciled by the condensed force of the words in which it finds expression. Intense as the feeling is, it cannot altogether resist the soothing influences of the Christmas bells, in virtue especially of the memories with which they are linked.

> " But they my troubled spirit rule,
> For they controlled me when a boy ;
> They bring me sorrow touched with joy,
> The merry, merry bells of Yule."

Students of Goethe will remember how it was the sound of the chimes of Easter and the choral song which interrupted Faust, as he was putting the cup of poison to his lips. The poet makes him say :

> "What hollow humming, what a sharp clear stroke
> Drives from my lips the goblets at their meeting ? "

XXIX.

THE USUAL CHRISTMAS OBSERVANCES UNCON-
GENIAL, BUT STILL HONORED FOR USE AND
WONT'S SAKE.

How " keep our Christmas-eve " when, in the absence of the friend whose presence had so often brightened it, there is " such compelling cause to grieve;" such cause, that is, as really leaves the mind no liberty to do aught but grieve, thus day by day "vexing"—a fine use of the word—ruffling or disturbing "household peace," here obviously the quiet family happiness; and *chaining* "regrets to his decease;" another felicitous use of metaphor. Then the wonted observances shall be omitted? No,

> "Yet go, and while the holly boughs
> Entwine the cold baptismal font,

referring to the customary decoration of the church at the Christmas season,

> Make one wreath more for Use and Wont,"

here personified, and characterized in the next stanza as

> "Old sisters of a day gone by,
> Gray nurses, loving nothing new;
> . . . . .
> . . . They too will die."

The Poet in his present mood sees death putting his destroying finger on everything, but why cheat Use and Wont of their due "before their time?"

XXX.

"CHRISTMAS-DAY — SUCCESSIVE MOODS — FORCED MIRTH SUCCEEDED BY TEARS, SILENCE AND THEN BY DEGREES SWEETER HOPE." F.W.R.

The customary celebration of Christmas goes on. The sense of loss runs through it all, making the show of gladness a "vain pretence." Its joy is dimmed by "an awful sense of one mute Shadow watching all." The day itself is dull, and wet, and wintry, as if in sympathy with their despondent feeling. The succession of moods in the poem is natural, and is finely depicted; first, silent looks in one another's faces, contrasting with the winds which swept "the winter land," then song, impetuous because forced, then a gentler feeling, induced by the thought—surely not without connection with the Christmas story—"They rest, their sleep is sweet," out of which there rises a new and higher note of gladness;

" . . . they do not die,
Nor lose their mortal sympathy,
Nor change to us, although they change."

Their change means "gathered power," and the

spirit, freed from its burden of clay, "the keen, seraphic flame," pierces "from orb to orb, from veil to veil."

Here for the first time in the Poem, the long monody of grief is broken by the note of hope and of joy; the lost presence, "the vanished life" is recovered; extinguished here, it flames yonder; lost to sight, it is restored to faith. Two points should not be overlooked at this stage. First, it is surely not incidental that the attainment, or at least the expression, of this conviction, is made coincident with the sound of the Christmas bells. We seem entitled to say that the Poet's hope of immortality is primarily based on Revelation, that the light which illumines or at least relieves for him the otherwise black darkness of the grave is kindled at the cradle of Bethlehem. It is important to become seized of this truth, since more than one of his commentators seem determined to make his belief in immortality, so far as In Memoriam goes, simply and solely the outgrowth of his inward feeling, the postulate, as it were, of that love which is felt to be undying, immortal; whereas that is rather to be regarded as the weapon with which he fights the doubts of his age, doubts in which he himself may have sometimes shared. In any case, it cannot be said to be the exclusive ground of the hope of the Hereafter which comes to light in the Poem. Second, the hope of immortality which rises in the night of this household's sorrow, is a hope which embraces others, as well as the loved one whose withdrawal had darkened for a time their Christmas gladness. It is his personal loss which the Poet has hitherto bewailed. It is the recovery of others besides—of all—which he now sings. "*They do not die.*" In the very nature of the case, it must be so. The loss to any of us, of child, or brother, or friend, is a purely personal matter; the hope, kindled at the altar of Revelation, which gives us that child, or brother, or friend back, must ever include others also. The grief is personal, the consolation general.

The new feeling finds noble and fitting expression in the lines :

> "Rise, happy morn, rise, holy morn,
>   Draw forth the cheerful day from night :
>   O Father, touch the east and light
> The light that shone when Hope was born."

XXXI.

Questions regarding the nature of the future state.

The fact of immortality being admitted, questions very naturally arise regarding its character; in particular regarding the state of the departed, the interest which they are permitted to take or are precluded from taking in those who are still living. The sequence of the poems is perfect at this point, and the new range of thought into which they are turned comes naturally. "Until now memory has brought the dead friend back into his old place, or sorrow has contemplated his place empty of him. Now faith follows him into his new being -and the contemplation of the unseen life begins." There is obvious propriety in taking Lazarus, whom Christ raised, as an example to bridge the path of enquiry from the world of sense to that of faith. He has been in both.

His case is one, the Poet says, which might conceivably have furnished answers to our curious but always baffled questionings regarding the place, and occupations of the departed, and doing which, it "had surely added praise to praise;" that is, as I understand it, had added the praise of extending man's knowledge of the future state, to the praise of restoring the loved brother from the tomb. In reality it has not done so; it has resolved for us no doubt, has shed no light on the impenetrable mystery involved in death.

> "Behold a man raised up by Christ !
> The rest remaineth unreveal'd ;
> He told it not ; or something seal'd
> The lips of that evangelist."

NOTE.—Dr. Gatty has a strange misinterpretation, or what seems such, of the words "Had surely added praise to praise;" making them to mean, "might have sealed and confirmed the promise that 'Blessed are the dead that die in the Lord.'" In such an interpretation, the language "added praise to praise" finds no explanation.

XXXII.

THE ENGROSSMENT AND DEVOTION OF LOVE AS EXEMPLIFIED IN MARY'S DEVOTION TO HER LORD.

The transition from Lazarus to Mary is a very natural one, on the supposition, which was the actual case here, that the author was in quest of spiritual truth. The piece supplies us with one of the most exquisite and touching, if not the most exquisite and touching, of all the poems in In Memoriam. Many may surpass it in grandeur and stateliness, in depth and brilliance of color, in the subtle interpenetration of nature and of human feeling; none surpasses it in condensed force and beauty; and no one equals it in the deep and sympathetic insight into the spiritual realm which it reveals. The poem is so lofty in thought as to impress the most unsusceptible ; so simple in expression as to be intelligible to the most unlettered; so exquisitely beautiful in form as to forbid the alteration of a single word. Such a picture of devout love as it forms will not fail to charm, we may believe, while the English tongue continues to be spoken, and the sense for the appreciation of spiritual truth and beauty survives among men.

The very first words arrest us by their exceeding depth and suggestiveness, and by what we may term the boldness as well as the beauty of the metaphor

"Her eyes are homes of silent prayer,"

the absorbing power of affection, especially of an affection which has the blessed Christ for its object follows.

"Nor other thought her mind admits
But, he was dead, and there he sits,
And He that brought him back is there.

CANTO XXXII. 71

> Then one deep love doth supersede
> All other, when her ardent gaze
> Roves from the living brother's face,
> And rests upon the Life indeed."

Then there is the utter gladness, unclouded by doubts and fears, which grows out of such devotion. The line

> "Whose loves in higher love endure,"

may perhaps require some explanation. It would seem to be equivalent to this: whose earthly attachments are not destroyed but are preserved and perfected in being taken up into the higher love which the devout soul cherishes towards God; in the case before us, that of Mary, whose love to a brother endures in her love to Him who had raised him from the tomb. Finally there is the self-possession, which is not effaced but is rather perfected, and blessedness with it, in the love which has the Life for its object.

> " What souls possess themselves so pure,
> Or is there blessedness like theirs?"

In the connection in which this poem stands, with curious and unanswered questions preceding it (xxxi.), and with the expression of grave and disquieting doubts following in one poem after another, it may have been the design of the poet, many are of opinion it was, to represent Mary as the picture of a person, in whose loving devotion to the Saviour and fellowship with Him, all fears in regard to the future are lost; "one, who has such satisfaction in the presence of the Life indeed, that curiosity about unseen things finds no place." Emerson is quoted as saying, "Of immortality, the soul when well employed, is incurious. It is so well, that it is sure it will be well. It asks no questions of the Supreme power."

XXXIII.

The danger of unsettling faith by detaching it from form.

This poem is one which requires careful interpretation. In it the Poet becomes the preacher. The person, whom he addresses, the representative of a class not indisposed to intellectual arrogance, is one who has laid aside the simple beliefs of his childhood, but who after a season of doubt and conflict has come to entertain what he regards as a more rational faith; a faith, for example, such as that of men, who recognize the spiritual element in man,

CANTO XXXIII. 73

who believe in a Supreme Power ruling the world in righteousness, in an ever-active Love guiding the meek and restoring the penitent, but who nevertheless refuse to accept the historic creeds of Christendom, or even to allow their sense of the divine and the spiritual to be embodied in any definite doctrinal statements whatever. A man of this class is said to be one

"Whose faith has centre everywhere."

The exact idea intended to be conveyed is not easily reached : perhaps it is that of stability, a faith not easily overturned ; well-poised, like a body in stable equilibrium. This characterization must be regarded as proceeding on the man's own estimate ; others might be disposed to substitute *nowhere* for "everywhere."

"Nor cares to fix itself to form."

"Form," as must be obvious from what has been already said, is in this connection, definite statement, distinctly articulated belief.

The Poet, without letting us see how far he sympathizes with the intellectual position, warns the man who occupies it, and who in doing so seems "to have reached a purer air," not to unsettle or disturb by "shadowed hint," by vague suggestions of doubt, the faith of his sister, who holds to the simple beliefs of her childhood, and thus

> ". . . confuse
> A life that leads melodious days,"

a felicitous description surely, embodying something of the melody of the life of which it speaks. With all her unacquaintance with the realm of philosophic thought into which he has risen,

> "Her hands are quicker unto good."

If right living, if prompt and active benevolence be the test, then her simpler and more definite faith is seen to have the advantage. The Poet goes on to say, with reference probably to the Incarnation, or, it may be to the Eucharist,

> "O sacred be the flesh and blood
> To which she links a truth divine."

In the closing stanza, the man who is disposed to look contemptuously on creeds or forms of belief, even Revelation itself, who counts it the part of ripened reason, to hold simply "by the law within," is reminded that his more rational faith, as he deems it, may leave his life a failure "in a world of sin."

> "And even for want of such a type."

"Such a type," that is, as the one divine and

spotless Life supplies. Most seasonable and necessary warning; the sublimated faith of the philosopher achieves few victories over "the world, the flesh and the devil."

Note.—Genung, who has written so fully on In Memoriam, and often to good purpose, is undoubtedly astray in his interpretation of this and the two preceding poems. "Lazarus and Mary," he remarks, "illustrate two phases of Christian life; those whose ripened reason and spiritual insight make their views of unseen things approach the character of knowledge, and those whose faith without knowledge supports itself by forms." Now one need not hesitate to say that the identification of Lazarus in Canto xxxi., or by implication in this Canto, with any such phase of religious life as that above indicated, is utterly groundless; while Mary even, with her eye on the personal Saviour, can with difficulty be regarded as the type of a faith which "supports itself by forms." Her's is much more a faith which is fed by love. One wonders to find this misinterpretation of Genung incorporated without remarks by Rolfe in his Annotated Edition of the Poem.

XXXIV.

The Christian Doctrine of Immortality Corroborated by the Facts of our own Moral Nature.

At this point in the Poem the question of immortality assumes a new phase; one in which it is contemplated again and again in the course of the Poem. It is discussed from the point of view of human reason, not from that of Revelation. The value of these discussions has been very differently estimated. Some, attracted mainly by literary beauty, rate them low;

others, yet more concerned with the truth, than with mere form, find in them the supreme interest of the Poem. There is evidence that the Poet threw into them his whole force, both of thought and of imagination; and in reality, be their value as contributions to the settlement of the great question of immortality what it may, there are no parts of In Memoriam which shew greater intensity of feeling and greater force of expression.

In this, then, and the following poem, the Poet finds himself for the first time face to face with the doubt of the age; and finds himself face to face with it to say that whatever show of truth it may possess, it is in conflict not less with the intuitions of reason, than with the teachings of Revelation. The denial of immortality, the total and final extinction of the personality in death, does not only impair the dignity and happiness of human life, it destroys its meaning, it renders human existence a hopeless enigma. Make this life all, that is, for a being such as man feels himself to be, endowed with conscience, with religious feelings, with the capacity of boundless love, and with eager yearnings after an ideal never quite realized here, then this green earth, that glowing sun is not wise and ordered grace, it is "fantastic beauty," like that which is seen on the frosted pane, or

> " . . . such as lurks
> In some wild poet, when he works
> Without a conscience or an aim."

The lofty conception which Tennyson has of his art, so conspicuous in his poetry, and differentiating it from not a little of the literature of the day, comes out incidentally here.

Religion likewise, on the supposition that death ends all, has no longer any meaning, or, at least, any attraction. "What then were God to such as I?" Suicide is the only wisdom.

> "'Twere best at once to sink to peace,
> Like birds the charming serpent draws,
> To drop head-foremost in the jaws
> Of vacant darkness and to cease."

Substantially the same plea for immortality is made again and again in the course of the Poem, and it is made with an urgency, with an almost passionate vehemence, explained at once by the supreme interest which attaches to the truth, and by the prevalence, and the plausibility of materialistic views of man and of human destiny. The argument is not to be misunderstood. It is not of the logical or the scientific kind. It is based on the possession by man of an intellectual and moral nature. To such a being, the world, human life, must be rational, must be righteous. It has ceased to be either, if death is the extinction of personal existence.

XXXV.

IMMORTALITY THE CONDITION OF ANY LOVE THAT IS WORTHY OF THE NAME.

This poem is in some respects the converse of the former. The supposition is made in it, that the hope of a life beyond the grave is extinguished, at least, that all probabilities are against it, the sorrowful conclusion to which some have come; what then? Is the sweetness of love, even though to be tasted only for a brief hour, not itself enough to make life a blessing and a joy?

> "Might I not say, 'Yet even here,
> But for one hour, O Love, I strive,
> To keep so sweet a thing alive?'"

No; for, first, the sweetness would change, would all but vanish, in view of the contrast between the fleeting life allotted to Love, and the unending play of stream and ocean, which rises before the imagination. This seems to be the force of the third and fourth stanzas; a force, as far as one can learn, not very generally apprehended, or at least not very clearly expressed by the expositors of the Poem. But, second,

> ". . . if Death were seen
> At first as Death, Love had not been
> Or been in narrowest working shut;"

if there were no instinct of immortality in man's breast, either Love would not arise, or it would be a mere coarse and sensual passion; like that of the satyr in the woods. In other words, the nobility of love, and as the poet will say, of life, depends on the belief in immortality; Genung says "in its own immortality."

The meaning of this poem, it may be observed, has been mistaken by one who not seldom shews a great measure both of learning and insight in his treatment of In Memoriam: Brother Azarias. He remarks on the poem: "Going deeper still, Tennyson finds in the love he bears his friend,—in all true love—an argument for his immortality." In this canto, and at this stage of the poem, there is no such argument. It is less surprising to find Genung making the same mistake.

"Æonian hills" (3rd stanza); everlasting hills or hills enduring for ages. The word seems to be one of the poet's coining.

"Forgetful shore" (4th stanza); a shore on which all is so changeful that it can retain no memory of the past—none of those who have lived and loved upon it.

Note.—It may not be amiss to transfer to these pages the following striking argument for immortality, somewhat analogous to that of the poet and quoted by Tainsh: "Thus if the celestial hope be a delusion, we plainly see who are the mistaken. Not the mean and grovelling souls, who never reached so great a thought, not the drowsy and easy natures, who are content with the sleep of sense through life, and the sleep of darkness ever after, not the selfish and pinched of conscience, of small thought and smaller love—no, these, in such case, are right, and the universe is on their miserable scale. The deceived are the great and holy, whom all men, ay, these very insignificants themselves, revere; the men who have lived for something better than their happiness and spent themselves on the race or fallen at the altar of human good. . . . Whom are we to revere, and what can we believe, if the inspirations of the highest of created natures are but cunningly devised fables?"

XXXVI.

Despite man's instinctive and rational hope of immortality, the revelation of truth in Christ is needful and welcome.

The Poet's thoughts revert to Revelation, as if not altogether sure of the argument he has framed.

"Tho' truths in manhood darkly join
Deep-seated in our mystic frame."

The truths of religion, inclusive of the great

truth of immortality, are indeed found "in manhood," that is, in man's nature,—in the human mind and constitution,—rooted deeply in, stamped ineffaceably on, "our mystic" or mysterious "frame," but they are at the same time "darkly" joined, their subtle connections are far from clear; we welcome Him, therefore, who embodied them "in a tale"—either with a reference to the Saviour's so frequent use of parable in inculcating truth, or more probably to the story itself of His own life on earth—and thus made them, not the privileged possession of the few thinkers of the race, but the common heritage, the "current coin" of mankind.

To meet the need arising from the fact that "Wisdom," Divine Wisdom, had to deal with mortal powers, to which "closest words" fail to reveal truth, the Word had breath, "the Word was made flesh and dwelt amongst men," John 1 : 14,

" . . . and wrought
With human hands the creed of creeds
In loveliness of perfect deeds,
More strong than all poetic thought ; "

which all can understand; the reaper in the harvest field (notice the poet's love of the concrete), the mason on the wall, the digger by the grave,

> "And those wild eyes, that watch the wave
> In roarings round the coral reef."

"Closest words" (2nd stanza); words fitting the truth in the closest way.

"Wild eyes" (4th stanza); "Wild" either as the eyes of savages, or, which is to be preferred, the eyes of those who watch the waves, which threaten to wreck the boats and engulph their loved ones.

XXXVII.

IS SUCH RECOURSE IN HIS SONG TO REVEALED TRUTH NOT A PROFANATION?

This again is a chorus song, one in which the Poet reflects on and characterizes his work rather than gives expression to his sentiments either regarding his friend, or regarding the momentous questions which his death had raised. It is important, moreover, as throwing light on what he counted his proper sphere as a poet.

Urania, the heavenly Muse, is represented as rebuking him for his intrusion into the field of Revelation, within which others could speak to greater profit, and as bidding him go to Parnassus, the poet's hill, and there win his laurel wreath through the lips of his own " earthly

Muse," Melpomene. He accepts the rebuke and answers,

> " I am not worthy even to speak
> Of thy prevailing mysteries ; "

but Arthur loved to speak " of things divine," and recalling what he said,

> " I murmured *as I came along*
> Of comfort clasped in truth reveal'd ; "

leading us to understand that his entrance into the field of Revelation was incidental, and not in the main line of the task which he had set himself.

> " And loiter'd in the Master's field
> And darken'd sanctities with song."

He is so far from claiming to shed light on Revelation, that he feels his song rather darkens the sacred truths taught by Christ. It is the fact, nevertheless, that the poetry of Tennyson evinces a minute acquaintance with the Scriptures, and that he has known how to borrow from them many a bold metaphor and many a striking allusion.

"Prevailing mysteries " (3rd stanza); with reference probably to the power or force which these mysteries exerted on the minds of men.

"Dear to me as sacred wine;" in the first edition, "dear as sacramental wine."

XXXVIII.

HIS GRIEF REMAINS OR REAPPEARS SLIGHTLY SOLACED BY SONG.

It is springtime, but the reviving life of nature cannot make itself felt in his life; it awakens no responsive movement there. He drags along the journey of life "with weary steps," and "always under altered skies," the horizon narrowed or rather "gone," as in the case of one hemmed in with darkness; the purple vanished from the heavens. In the music of the birds,

> "The herald melodies of spring,"

there is for him no more joy; but a gleam, "a doubtful" or fitful "gleam of solace lives" in his song "which it may be—it may be—that Arthur hears" (Chapman), and if he does,

> "Then are these songs I sing of thee
> Not all ungrateful to thine ear."

"The blowing season" (2nd stanza); that is, the blooming season. Comp. German "blühen."

"Spirits render'd free" (3rd stanza); emancipated from the body, viewed as a clog or hindrance.

XXXIX.

THE YEW TREE WITH ITS SCARCELY PERCEPTIBLE BLOSSOMS AND SOON RETURNING TO ITS NATIVE GLOOM, IMAGES HIS DOUBTFUL AND FLEETING SOLACE.

This poem did not appear in the first editions of In Memoriam. It was added in the edition which appeared in 1869. It is very generally regarded as one of the more obscure pieces of the work. It is addressed, like ii., to the yew tree, with whose "stubborn hardihood" of gloom, the poet at an earlier stage had felt himself to be in sympathy, or which he desired to share. It blossoms and forms seeds like other trees. Being springtime, the blossom is on it. To it, too, has come "the golden hour." Of it, or rather, to it, he says:

> "And answering now my random stroke
> With fruitful cloud and living smoke;"

The meaning is, that when the tree receives "a random" shake, or "stroke," it sheds the pollen like dust; a "fruitful cloud" as fertilizing the ovules or rudimentary seed, "living smoke," as containing in it the element or principle of life. But sorrow, it is said, whispered from her lying lips, addressing the tree,

> "Thy gloom is kindled at the tips
> And passes into gloom again."

Considering that these lines state a simple and undeniable fact in the case of the yew tree, why is Sorrow said to speak it with "lying lips?" The answer, so far as we can see, must be this, that it is supposed to carry the suggestion that his "sorrow," now "touched with joy," must end in gloom after all.

XL.

THE BRIDE'S PARTING FROM HER HOME COMPARED TO AND CONTRASTED WITH THE PARTING IN DEATH.

The comparison is a natural one, and it is wrought out with great skill and beauty of detail, and with deep and tender feeling. There are points of resemblance between the two cases. There is in both the severance of old and cherished ties, separation attended with more or less of sorrow, even in the case of the bride;

> " . . hopes and light regrets that come
> Make April of her tender eyes;
>
> And doubtful joys the father move,
> And tears are on the mother's face."

There is in both, too, an important purpose to be served; in her case, to rear, to teach a new generation, in his to discharge "the great offices that suit the full grown energies of heaven." But there is a point of difference likewise, and that is the outstanding feature in the picture; it is here the tender and exquisite pathos of the poem reaches its climax. Her separation from the old home is not absolute—is not for ever.

> "Ay me, the difference I discern!
> How often shall her old fireside
> Be cheer'd with tidings of the bride,
> How often she herself return.
>
> But thou and I have shaken hands,
> Till growing winters lay me low;
> My paths are in the fields I know,
> And thine in undiscover'd lands."

How intense the sense of separation in the last stanza; how simply and touchingly expressed!

Note.—Genung makes the theme of this poem, "Progress in another world, illustrated in the life of a bride, who leaves her parental home and becomes the centre of a new family circle, and so an agent in the world's progress. Such progress, only nobler is in heaven." This, as it appears to me, is an arbitrary and forced interpretation and receives any color of support from the poem itself, only by making the 5th stanza, which contains simply a subsidiary point in the comparison, the governing one in the whole poem. A reader who has no theory to support, who is not bent on discovering connections where none exist, will readily feel that the whole emphasis of the poem lies, not in the resemblances noted, but in the difference. The very first line, when rightly understood, "Could we forget," etc. *i.e.*, O that we could forget, etc., disproves the view of Genung.

XLI.

THE FEAR OF ETERNAL SEPARATION FROM HIS FRIEND ARISING BECAUSE OF THE START HE HAS GOT.

With this poem there commences a series of questionings regarding the nature of the future life, and the condition of the departed therein. This is the subject of the poems from xli. to xlvii. A variety of suppositions are brought under review. In the poem before us, the future state is regarded as one of constant, upward progress, and, the whole problem of immortality being in the meantime considered mainly as it affects his relation to his friend, the fear thence arises, that he cannot again share his companionship.

It will be noted, that in the poem immortality is assumed as a fact, but it is also a fact that the two are parted. Shall they ever meet again, or, must their unequal attainments not keep them forever separate? Arthur's course on earth was ever upward, like altar-fire. His spirit ever rose

> "As flies the lighter thro' the gross."

But that upward course could be followed; now it can be traced no longer. "I have lost the links that bound thy changes," that is, that mark the limits of thy advance. The wish arises, (he knows it to be foolish and impracticable) that by an effort of will he could

> " . . leap the grades of life and light,"

which now separate them

> "And flash at once, my friend to thee."

Mrs. Chapman, generally so sane in her interpretation of the Poem, is surely at fault here, in regarding these lines as a cry for death on the part of the Poet.

The wish thus expressed, incapable of gratification, leaves him the prey of the chilling doubt, which haunts him like a spectre; that he cannot again be the mate of Arthur, but, despite all his striving, must forever remain a life behind; that differences of attainment, acting like a power of gravitation, must keep them in different spheres.

On the supposition of immortality, the fear thus expressed, must be pronounced not unnatural. Our ignorance of the conditions of the future life, makes it impossible for us to say, whether it is well or ill grounded.

"The howlings from forgotten fields" (4th stanza). The expression is an obscure one. Dr. Gatty remarks regarding it, there is "probably a classical allusion to those fields of mystic horror over which the spirits of the departed were supposed to range, uttering wild shrieks and cries."

"The secular to be," (6th stanza), denotes, the future ages.

XLII.

This fear overcome by the recollection, that inequality of mind did not separate them on earth.

Here, in the earthly life, Arthur "still outstript" him "in the race," and yet their companionship was intimate and happy. "Unity of place" united them, inequality of attainment

CANTO XLII.

notwithstanding. And "Place" (though how far place or locality applies to the future life is perhaps a moot point) may still "retain" or unite them, though more than ever unequal. After all, this inequality, the lofty attainments of his friend, now become "a lord of large experience" may only enhance the pleasure, for

> " . . what delights can equal those
> That stir the spirit's inner deeps,
> When one that loves, but knows not, reaps
> A truth from one that loves and knows,"

as it must increase the gain; for it will be then in his power to "train, to riper growth the mind and will," that is, his (the Poet's) mind and will.

The last two lines of the poem deserve attention. The thought is as just and winsome, as the expression is simple and beautiful.

The poem, it may be observed, affords an illustration of the idealizing process which so often goes on, when death removes a loved friend. A note contained in Dr. Gatty's "Key to In Memoriam" and giving Tennyson's own words, says expressly that Hallam looked up to him fully as much as he looked up to Hallam. A different explanation, indeed, would be given by "Brother Azarias" who says, "Precisely as the 'I' of the poem came to stand for the whole human race, even so the 'Arthur' of the poem has become idealized into the representative of all that is or could be excellent in a deceased friend." Of the former we have the assurance from the Poet himself; of the latter he gives us no hint. The two things are very far from being necessarily connected. The admission of the latter, if one reflects on what is implied in it, would completely alter the situation depicted in the poem. The presence, from which the Poet dreads difference of attainment is to separate him forever, is not that of "the representative of all that is or could be excellent in a deceased friend," it is that of his personal friend, his "more than brother" invested indeed by his imagination with new and higher excellence.

Note.—Genung gives the force of the poem in these words: "This fear allayed by the thought of love. Here on earth he was always far ahead, yet always helpful; so there, where progress is certainly progress in love, he will all the more surely devote himself to the late-coming friend as guide and teacher." This is, as any careful reader will see, an example, not a few of which Genung supplies, of reading into a poem, a meaning which it does not contain, and which, so far as one can judge from the words used, the Poet never intended to express.

XLIII.

Death viewed as a long, unconscious trance, and love re-awakening with returning life.

The fear expressed in xli., it has been observed, "was not quite that of the loss of all communion whatsoever, but that of the loss of equal matehood" (Tainsh). That proceeds on the idea, that there is no interruption in death to progress, or, rather it implies, that it proceeds at an accelerated space.

Another conception altogether of the future state comes into view in this poem, and is treated with all the author's poetic skill; the conception, namely, that the state to which death introduces its subject, and which lasts until the resurrection of the body, is one of unconsciousness. The spirit exists, but exists in a state of unconscious trance. This view of the intermediate state, as is well known, is one which has been widely entertained both in earlier and later times. Our Poet neither accepts nor rejects it. He simply deals with it according to his method, as one of the possibilities arising out of death.

It does not seem to have had much attraction for his mind, as he does not return to it. It has even been made a ground of complaint against him, that the prevailing view of the future state, contained in In Memoriam, is that of one of active and continuous progress, to the disregard of what is claimed to be the Christian doctrine of Paradise. "The Christian faith concerning the blessed dead," says Tainsh, "is that neither are they fully awake nor do they wholly sleep. . . . They sleep to rest; they wake to love and long." Thus only, it is claimed, does "the resurrection of the body" come to its true significance.

It is not necessary that we should pronounce an opinion on this point. It is sufficient to note that the view of the intermediate state dealt with in this poem is, as we have seen, that of a state of sleep or unconsciousness. It is interesting to notice how such a view is regarded by the Poet, who throughout the Poem habitually looks at the question of the Hereafter, not in its broad and general bearing, but as affecting his relationship to his friend.

Well, if this were the true account, it would be the negation of progress for the time being; it would not necessarily be the destruction, or even the impairment of love, but only the suspension of its exercise. The soul will awake in the resurrection from its long sleep and Love will awake with it. On this supposition, the spirit will continue to slumber

> "Thro' all its intervital gloom,"

"the gloom," that is, resting on it between the two lives, that prior to death, and that subsequent to resurrection; its "bloom" acquired or displayed here, not lost, but simply "folded." In that case, nothing is really lost in death. There is no disintegration of spiritual fibre, no blanching even of color. In this "still," speechless "garden of the souls" the entire realm of human experience survives, wrapt up "in many a figured leaf." Love, too, the love which lent nobility and sweetness to life, survives; not indeed in active exercise, but in potential; and will at the soul's springtime, here termed "the spiritual prime,"

> "Rewaken with the dawning soul."

The conception, it will be seen, is one wrought out with great skill and in a poem of exquisite beauty; the metaphor of the soul, as a flower, is maintained throughout with complete consistency in all the details of the picture. The condensed force and beauty of the following expressions will be noted : The "spirit's folded bloom," "the sliding hour," "silent traces of the past," "the still garden of the souls," "a figured leaf enrolls." We have next another companion poem, growing out of this one.

XLIV.

Death being viewed as on the whole a state of oblivion, may it not, however, be visited by gleams of recollection ?

Any light on the subject of the character of the after life, apart from that which comes through Revelation, must be borrowed from, or at least in some way connected with, our experience in the present earthly state of existence. Well,

" . . here the man is more and more,"

i.e. accumulates knowledge, exists in a state of continuous progress. But with his growth in knowledge, there is conjoined the loss of recollection of some prior state of being ;

" But he forgets the days before
God shut the doorways of his head."

This singular and unquestionably obscure expression, " before God shut the doorways of his head," has been interpreted as meaning, before the skull of the infant is closed. The forgetfulness in that case would be forgetfulness of the very earliest stages of infancy, extending perhaps even to the purely sensational experiences in the womb. Or, the Platonic doctrine of preëxistence, the fact of a preëxistent state of being, out of which the soul comes in birth into the present, may be, probably is, the supposition with which the Poet is dealing ; and in that case, the forgetfulness would denote the total or all but total disappearance from memory of everything connected with that prior state. We say "all but total" disappearance, for he qualifies it in a way.

> " And yet perhaps the hoarding sense
> Gives out, at times, (he knows not whence,)
> A little flash, a mystic hint."

Many have spoken, Bacon, among others, of experiences of the kind described in these words, vague recollections, which refusing connection with or explanation by, anything in the present life, seem to come from some earlier and entirely forgotten state of being. The Poet now makes fine and happy use of this obscure and strange experience, plays with it, so to say, to bring his vanished friend once more into touch with him. The state of oblivion, regarded for the moment, as that of the departed, may in like manner be relieved or interrupted in his friend's case, by "some dim touch of earthly things." If so, addressing him, he says :

"O, turn thee round, resolve the doubt,"

" the doubt," that is, as to whence the " touch " comes, and what it means ;

" My guardian angel will speak out
In that high place, and tell thee all."

The exposition of this poem would not be complete, without subjoining what Tennyson says in " The two voices ; "

" Moreover something is or seems,
That touches me with mystic gleams,
Like glimpses of forgotten dreams

Of something felt, like something here,
Of something done, I know not where,
Such as no language may declare,"

and these four lines from Wordsworth's fine ode, " Intimations of Immortality."

" Our birth is but a sleep and a forgetting ;
The soul that rises with our life's star,
Hath had elsewhere its setting,
And cometh from afar."

XLV.

The bearing of the sense of individuality acquired in this life, on the question of memory in another.

In the earliest stages of human life the sense of individuality or personal being, the sense of the "me," is wanting. The life of the infant is one of pure sensibility. The subject has not learned to distinguish itself from things around it. The self-conscious "I" is as yet undeveloped. The process of its formation is described in this poem. It is termed rounding "to a separate mind," a mind, that is, consciously distinguished from the things which it sees and touches, and is said to be accomplished by or "thro' the frame that binds him in." Whatever may be the case with the Divine Personality, the sense of our own arises through limitation, through the physical frame which separates us from other persons and from everything around. Further, once acquired, it cannot be unlearned or forfeited.

But what has all this to do with the subject of present interest to the Poet, the character of the future state? Just this, he grounds on it an argument, or at least he finds in it a presumption in favor of the view that man carries the individuality, or sense of personal identity thus gained, unshattered across the boundary which separates this life from another, and with it, therefore, the recollection of the earthly past.

> "This use may lie in blood and breath,
> Which else were fruitless of their due,
> Had man to learn himself anew
> Beyond the second birth of death."

The argument as presented in the poem, for the existence of memory in another state of being, may not seem to carry much weight to some. After all, it will be observed, that the Poet does not claim for it more than a conditional or contingent force. "This use *may* lie in blood and breath."

XLVI.

ON THE SUPPOSITION OF MEMORY SURVIVING IN THE FUTURE STATE, THE WHOLE PAST EARTHLY LIFE MUST STAND DISCLOSED TO IT.

This again is somewhat of a companion poem to the preceding; on which, however, it takes a step in advance, claiming for the immortal dead a clear knowledge of their entire past. Much is forgotten, passes out of view in this life. Speaking of himself and his friend, he says :

> "The path we came by, thorn and flower,
> Is shadowed by the growing hour,"

that is, by the lengthening day of life, and for the good reason, that life may not fail, by indulging in retrospect. Forgetting the past is even one of the conditions of progress here. Only thus can the present get its due.

But there, where character is perfected, "no shade can last." The entire past of the life must stand disclosed, and in it, "those five years of friendship," "its richest field."

The last stanza is somewhat difficult. The reference in the first two lines would seem to be to those five short years in which he had enjoyed the friendship of Arthur. But if this were the whole domain of Love, he must say :

> "O Love! thy province were not large,
> A bounded field, nor stretching far ; '

he will therefore have love widen its domain, brighten with its roseate hues the whole of his life.

"Look also," that is, appear, shew thyself, O Love,

> " . . . a brooding star,
> A rosy warmth from marge to marge

'So that (to him) looking back upon this life from out the clearness and the calm of the other, it may appear all tinged with roseate hues of love—all—not the five rich years of friendship only."—(Mrs. Chapman).

> Dr. Gatty is almost certainly wrong in his interpretation of the words "lest life should fail in looking back." His rendering is, "the past becomes mercifully shaded, as time goes on, otherwise the retrospect would be intolerable;" most true, but a truth not meant here, not suitable to the context.

XLVII.

The idea of the absorption of the individual soul in universal being repudiated.

This poem takes up and looks at, especially in the light of Love, another possibility in regard to the future life; that, viz., according to which personality—as dependent on "temporary and probably physical conditions"—is lost in death, and the individual soul is merged in the general soul, or in universal being. This doctrine, or one like it, with modifications in some instances, that wear a very Christian guise, has been widely held. The Poet's account of it is remarkably fine, all the more that it is made in terms already employed to describe the rise of self-conscious personality.

> "That each who seems a separate whole,
>   Should move his rounds;

"rounds" must mean here that which rounds him off from other beings, and at the same time rounds him in. (Compare the use of the word in xlv., l. 9).

> ". . . and fusing all
>   The skirts of self again, should fall
> Remerging in the general soul."

The Poet pronounces this, a "faith as vague as all," *i.e.*, altogether, "unsweet." The absorption of the individual in universal being, even in the God of Pantheism, is really the equivalent of extinction; it certainly does away with the possibility of that recognition or companionship in the future state which Love demands. But no;

> "Eternal form shall still divide
>   The eternal soul from all beside;
> And I shall know him when we meet."

Some "vaster dream" as to the life beyond may be conceivable, such as that of the absorption of all in God, but if it took away the possibility of mutual recognition and fellowship, it could not "hit the mood of Love on earth."

And yet the alternative is not absolutely

and decisively rejected. As a final fancy and that Love may play with it, he for a moment admits the supposition of absorption in the Soul of the universe; but doing so, "he holds love to be so strong and so persistent that the spirit of his friend would await his own, to clasp it and bid it farewell before losing itself in light."

> " . . . He seeks at least
> Upon the last and sharpest height,
> Before the spirits fade away,
> Some landing place to clasp and say,
> ' Farewell! we lose ourselves in light.' "

The Poet's own rendering of these lines, as given by Dr. Gatty, is: "If indeed we are to be merged in the universal soul, let us have at least one more parting, before we lose our individualities in the Great Being," (p. 52).

XLVIII.

THESE SONGS ARE MUSINGS ON DEATH AND IMMORTALITY, NOT CONCLUSIVE INTELLECTUAL PROOFS.

This and the following poem may be regarded as another pair of chorus poems. They aim at characterizing his song rather than expressing either his thought or his feeling, though this statement does not apply without qualification to the second, as the closing stanza shews. Moreover, they are both slightly apologetic in their tone. "These brief lays of sorrow born" are not meant to give conclusive answers to the great questions raised by death. In that case men might well scorn them. The concern of Sorrow is not "to part" the false from the true, "and prove," establish something certain regarding, the Hereafter; but rather, when some "slender shade of doubt flits" before it, is suggested from without or arises from within, to take it and play with it, as Love may direct, thus making "it vassal unto Love," do Love service, in furnishing her with material for her song. But in thus sporting with words, Sorrow has her limits, which in her utterances, she would count it profanation to pass. These lays, at least, are but

"Short swallow flights of song, that dip
Their wings in tears and skim away."

The characterization is as beautiful and vivid as it is appropriate to the character of the poems which constitute In Memoriam.

"A slender shade of doubt" (2nd stanza); that is, some view regarding the future state, which, while not certain, has still something to say for itself.

XLIX.

THEY (THE SONGS) BORROW THEIR VARYING FORMS FROM ART, NATURE AND PHILOSOPHY; BENEATH THEM ALL LIE HIS DEEPER SORROWS UNEXPRESSED.

This poem, too, is apologetic ; it admonishes the reader in what light to regard his songs. " The subjects are deep and solemn, but blame not the muse for her temerity in touching them. She ventures but at the impulse of love, and questions rather than answers ; seeks to learn more than to teach," (Tainsh). The movements of thought and feeling which they reflect come from varied quarters : from Art, from Nature, from Philosophy and Science (the Schools). These movements coming in chance ways and at chance times, the Poet welcomes, as supplying new suggestions to Love, while musing on the Hereafter. They break upon the " sullen surface " of his sorrow, " chequering and dimpling it, like shafts of light and tender breezes playing upon a pool." (Chapman). The reader is to take a passing look ;

" Look thy look and go thy way,"

at this play of fancy which gleams in his song, but not to blame "the seeming wanton ripple; the fancies of the poet obey no law. After all it is but the surface play of feeling which is revealed,

> "Beneath all fancied hopes and fears;"

that is, beneath all the hopes and fears of fancy which have found expression in his songs;

> "Ay me! the sorrow deepens down,
> Whose muffled motions blindly drown
> The bases of my life in tears."

It seems correct to say that as the former chorus poem closed a series (xli.–xlvii.) occupied exclusively with questions regarding the state of the departed, so this one introduces another series (l.–lix.) predominantly, though not exclusively, taken up with the development, character and destiny of "the imperfect and sinful life of earth" under the influence of sorrow. It is charged throughout with, if possible, more intense feeling than the former.

"Like light in many a shiver'd lance" (1st stanza). The comparison is a striking one. The gleam of the wavelet on the pool, broken by the breeze, is compared to that of a lance broken to shivers, every separate fragment of which gleams.

"To make the sullen surface crisp" (2nd stanza); that is, to make it curl.

L.

THE IDEAL, OR SPIRITUAL PRESENCE OF HIS FRIEND, INVOKED TO BRIGHTEN AND TO CALM THE DARKER AND MORE DISQUIETING PASSAGES OF LIFE.

These darker passages are times of depression, his "light is low," "the blood creeps, the nerves prick and tingle, and the heart is sick;" times of fierce, feverish pain, on witnessing the wild work of death,

> "Time a maniac scattering dust,
> And Life, a Fury, slinging flame,"

(powerful metaphors); times of doubt, "when my faith is dry," like a channel deserted of its waters; times of pessimistic thought, when human life seems to have lost all nobleness, and men are like "flies of latter spring"

> "That lay their eggs, and sting and sing,
> And weave their petty cells and die,"

and last, not least, the hour of death,

> "on the low, dark verge of life,
> The twilight of eternal day."

Death, it will be noticed, is regarded as the end, "the term" of human conflict, and "the dark verge of life," as "the twilight of eternal day." This was no doubt the settled mind of the Poet regarding death, though at times in his case, as in the case of so many, it had to maintain itself amid conflict with doubt and fear.

The poem cannot be called a pleasant one; but it is an extremely strong and vivid picture of one of the darker moods which are liable to enter into human experience.

"Men the flies of latter spring" (3rd stanza). The reference, from the connection in which the words occur, would seem to be to those writers who assail the common faith of Christendom, soon pass off the scene, but leave their venomous words behind them, to poison the souls of the unwary.

LI.

THIS PRESENCE NOT DREADED, EVEN IF EARTH'S VILENESS STANDS DISCLOSED TO IT.

This poem, it will be observed, is closely connected with the preceding one. The fear, that his friend's love for him, if the desire therein expressed were granted, would be lessened by the discovery of his less noble traits, is repelled as wronging the dead.

"Shall love be blamed for want of faith?"

In the connection, the love here must be, not his love for his friend, but his friend's love for him. "To doubt that they (the dead) can know us, and yet love, is to wrong them. For they are wise, with the wisdom of death, and pitiful with the large mercy of God." (Chapman). Compare the statement in 1 John iii.: 20, where the greatness of God is adduced not to aggravate, but rather to assuage, the heart's fears and self-accusings. But this is done, it must not be forgotten, in connection with and under the qualification of the presence, in those in regard to whom the reassuring words are spoken, of an affection of a specifically moral, or rather spiritual kind; love of the brethren, of the disciples of Christ, as such.

In any case not all would be prepared to make the prayer their own,

"Be near us when we climb or fall;"

while not a few would take exception to the view of God, by implication at least, as making "allowance for us all;" not on the ground that it unduly magnifies His mercy, for that reaches unto the heavens, but that in its mode of statement, it seems to leave the moral character of the mercy in doubt, and to forget that holiness is an attribute of God, not less than mercy, that his eyes are " eyes of judgment, as well as of charity."

Notice the expression, (and stanza), "I had such reverence for his blame."

LII.

DISQUIETED NEVERTHELESS BY THE CONSCIOUS PRESENCE OF EVIL IN HIS LIFE, HE IS ASSURED THAT THE SPIRIT OF TRUE LOVE IS NOT OFFENDED BY HUMAN FRAILTY.

This poem raises and discusses, as do the two which follow, the question of the function of evil in the world, so difficult and so perplexing to faith ; and the view to which it seems to incline is, the rather perilous one, that evil is only a transient phenomenon, a mere stage through which the feeble finite being must pass on his way to the attainment of good. The poem as a whole is complicated, and its transitions rather difficult of apprehension.

The image of his friend rises before him. He is conscious of loving him, but not adequately. To do that he would require to possess his qualities ; for adequate love, the love which is worthy of the name, reflects the perfections of the object loved. But

"The Spirit of true love replied;"

the plaintive song of love is not to be blamed, although sung by one very conscious of human frailty. That frailty is unavoidable in man's case. No ideal of goodness, which the mind may frame, not even the record of the one sinless life, that of the Saviour of the world, has power to keep "a spirit wholly true" to that ideal. This we understand to be the force of the interrogation in the 3rd stanza :

"So fret not, like an idle girl,"

"Abide," be patient. Life, even if unhappily "dashed with flecks of sin," will be found to have issued in something valuable,

"When time hath sunder'd shell from pearl,"

that is, not exactly, as Dr. Gatty has it, "when the flesh has left the soul free from its contaminating influence," but when in the course of years, and in the process of development, good has by degrees thrown off the attaching evil.

One is obliged to say that the moral note struck in this poem is not a very high one. Perhaps this was to be expected from the

underlying conception of evil. As a result, the
"wealth is gathered in" without either repent-
ance or reparation. The whole process, moreover, is purely natural.

LIII.

THE DANGER INVOLVED IN THE VIEW THAT
EVIL IS BUT A STAGE ON THE WAY TO GOOD,
AND IN SOME INSTANCES THE MEANS EVEN OF
PROMOTING GOOD.

or

"THE NEEDS-BE OF EVIL IS TRUTH IN THE RETRO-
SPECT, FALSEHOOD AND PERILOUS IN PROS-
PECT."—F.W.R.

The Poet now faces, as became him, the peril
of the doctrine to which he has given expression. Even if it has to be admitted, that there
are instances in which a youth full of excess
and folly, has ripened into a richer and better
manhood than one coldly virtuous from the
beginning—instances which seem to verify the
proverb—"the greater the sinner, the greater
the saint,"

" . . dare we to this fancy give?"

i.e., yield. The word was, in the earliest edition,
not "fancy," but "doctrine," in the sense of

opinion or view. Are we ready to assume the responsibility of saying that the wild oats of youthful sowing were needed to fertilize a soil, that might have otherwise remained barren?

> " . . who would preach it as a truth
> To those that eddy round and round?"

The Poet, seized of the danger, becomes the preacher, not too soon, not too decisively. There is in reality only one safe view to entertain—that evil is evil in youth and in age, and must be fought and shunned in both. The philosophy that tends in any degree to obliterate the distinction between evil and good may call itself or be called "divine;" it certainly does not lead to God, and just as certainly is it at war with all our best moral instincts;

> "Hold thou the good; define it well:
> For fear divine Philosophy
> Should push beyond her mark, and be
> Procuress to the Lords of Hell."

as it must at least in some instances be, in advocating or even in excusing youthful indulgence as the path to ultimate sanctity or goodness.

LIV.

The Trust Expressed of Good as the Final Goal of all Evil.

The connection between this poem and the preceding one is not a very close one; not so close as it might appear. It is true that the term "good" which is found in the closing stanza of the one, reappears in the opening line of the other; but, as must be evident, the word does not express precisely the same idea in each case. In the former it is strictly moral good,—" Hold thou the good;"—in the latter, the conception is more general. It is a good in which, as the second stanza shews, even the lower animals are contemplated as sharing—good in the widest sense of the word. The hope is expressed in the poem that somehow, somewhere, such good

> ". . . will be the final goal of ill."

In this connection various forms of ill, or evil, in the wide sense of the term, are enumerated: physical, "pangs of nature;" moral, "sins of will;" spiritual, "defects of doubt;" *i.e.*, defects growing out of doubt, or perhaps even constituted by doubt; even inherited weaknesses "taints of blood." The thought of the Poet then passes beyond man, to that physical nature which suffers with and like him, and having singled out one form of suffering and death after another, and pictured them in a manner singularly vivid and realistic, the hope is expressed, that no part of all this is aimless,

> "Or but subserves another's gain."

But that this will be the issue:

> "... that good shall fall
> At last—far off—at last, to all,
> And every winter change to spring,"

he does not *know*, he "can but trust;" the trust even becomes a "dream," and his song, a cry in the night, an infant's cry; so conscious is the Poet of the limitation of human knowledge as to the great mystery of suffering and of sin;

> "So runs my dream; but what am I?
> An infant crying in the night;
> An infant crying for the light:
> And with no language but a cry."[1]

The helplessness of man in presence of the mysteries of human existence has surely never found more touching utterance than in these now familiar lines.

---

[1] Compare cxxiv., line 19:—
"Then was I as a child that cries,
But crying knows his father near."

LV.

THE HOPE OF PERSONAL IMMORTALITY SHAKEN BY WHAT IS WITNESSED, THOUGH NOT QUITE OVERTHROWN.

It should be noticed that the question in this and the following poem is not exactly that of the preceding one, the development of good out of evil. It is rather that of individual immortality. It seems a strong point in support of this, that the desire that no life may be utterly extinguished, springs from that which is likest God in us, benevolence; but Nature, which is God's work, seems to give the lie to our expectation, so careless is she, of the individual life, while maintaining the species. Accordingly the Poet, witnessing her callous waste, falters "where" he "firmly trod," feels his confidence shaken in the truth that "good," at least in this sense of it, "will be the final goal of ill," and finally falls

> " Upon the great world's altar stairs
> That slope thro' darkness up to God."

There are few finer or more striking conceptions in In Memoriam or indeed in modern literature, than that embodied in these lines.

It is not, however, easy to define exactly the meaning they were intended to convey. It is doubtful whether Davidson hits it. His words are: "Grandly original is the thought that this stair is an 'altar stair,' and that the great world itself is an altar upon which everything that lives, if it will save its life, must offer itself in sacrifice unto God." The idea of sacrifice seems entirely foreign to the passage. The attitude is rather one of worship or prayer, as that which befits the enquirer in such a realm, and in the maintenance of which light may be expected, if any, indeed, is to be given.

Another stanza follows, vividly depicting man's helplessness, in his attempt to solve the mystery of the Hereafter;

> "I stretch lame hands of faith, and grope,
> And gather dust and chaff;"

a vivid figurative characterization of all which his quest in this region brings him.

> " and call
> To what I feel is Lord of all,
> And faintly trust the larger hope."

As the alternatives before the mind of the Poet are, the extinction of individual being in death, or its prolongation after death, "the larger hope," in the connection in which it is here used, would naturally be regarded as denoting the latter simply. In reality, as now used, it has come to designate the ultimate salvation of the whole race of mankind, as distinguished from that of a certain number only ; a view, with which, we are not left in doubt, Tennyson entirely sympathized.

LVI.

THE HOPE OF IMMORTALITY STILL FARTHER DISCREDITED, OR "THE HIDEOUS 'NO' OF NATURE."—F.W.R.

The Poet is still interrogating nature. Her answer is that not only individual existences out of number have perished, but that whole species are extinct ;

> " A thousand types are gone ; "

I know nothing of immortality, " I bring to life, I bring to death ; " death with me ends all.

But imagine this to hold good of man ; man, with his faculty of worship, " who rolled the psalm to wintry skies ; " "wintry," *i.e.*, on the supposition that there is no God and no Hereafter ; " who built him fanes of fruitless prayer;" "fruitless," *i.e.*, on the like supposition; man, with his trust in Love, as at the heart of things, as the sovereign Power; with his lofty ideals and self-sacrificing efforts,

> "Who loved, who suffered countless ills,
> Who battled for the True, the Just."

Imagine this to hold good of him; accept the conclusion that for him, too, there is nothing beyond death; then so far as man is concerned, life is a monstrous incongruity, a horrible dream, an intolerable discord : then "dragons" of the prime," that is, of the earliest period of the earth's history,

> "That tare each other in their slime,
> Were mellow music match'd with him."

This poem is really, at least so it seems to me, one of the most powerful pleas for personal immortality, outside of Revelation. The plea is obviously grounded on the moral and religious nature which man possesses, and by the possession of which he is differentiated from all around him. That he should have no different end from the brute, should perish like it, is unnatural. Man's rational nature demands that the universe to which he stands related and of which he forms part, should be rational, but

CANTO LVI.

rational it does not appear to be, if a being so loftily endowed, capable of fellowship with God, who has in prayer actually participated in that fellowship, has no higher destiny than to "be blown about the desert dust, or sealed within the iron hills."

Still the agony remains ; for on such a question, for all highest natures, for such natures, especially in seasons of bereavement, doubt is agony. Out of this agony the prayer rises,

> "O for thy voice to soothe and bless !
> What hope of answer, or redress ?
> Behind the veil, behind the veil."

The meaning of the last two lines would seem to be, not so much that Revelation must solve the doubt, (though, as we have seen, Tennyson was a believer in Revelation and evidently, as his Memoir shows, knew its comfort), as that conclusive knowledge on the question of immortality, must come from one who has passed "behind the veil ;" or rather, will be reached by us, when death shall tell us this secret as so many others.

We come now to a triad of Chorus songs, (lvii., lviii., and lix.), in which speculative thought wholly ceases. "It is as if the heart had grown weary with the strain, and fell back like a tired bird into the nest of its personal sorrow" (Tainsh).

Note.—In the Vision of Sin, an earlier Poem, these words occur, referring to the same subject :

" At last I heard a voice upon the slope
Cry to the summit, ' Is there any hope ? '
To which an answer pealed from that high land,
But in a tongue no man could understand,
And on the glittering limit, far withdrawn,
God made Himself an awful rose of dawn."

LVII.

Simple lamentation of the lost friend.

We encounter a marked change in the strain of In Memoriam at this point. The course of thought in the immediately preceding poems, in which the Poet's mind was fiercely agitated in regard to the question of human destiny, is broken off abruptly. In this lyric, which may possibly be addressed to his sister, he simply abandons himself to the sense of loss, the loss of half his life. At the same time, he finds some solace in the thought, that his friend is richly shrined in these Poems, which have been wrung from the heart of sorrow. He does not anticipate for them, however, the lasting memory they are likely to enjoy.

" But I shall pass, my work shall fail."

But while he lasts, there will stay with him the deathless memory of his friend's departure out of life.

> "Yet in these ears, till hearing dies,
> One set slow bell will seem to toll
> The passing of the sweetest soul
> That ever look'd with human eyes."

The lines seem vocal with the melody of the slow-pealing bell.

LVIII.

The first prelude of the note of joy.

This Poem opens with a comparison of the "greetings to the dead," the Ave, Ave, Adieu, Adieu, which have thus far been the burden of these songs, to the drop, drop, of some dank burial vault. As a result, the peace of other hearts had been idly, *i.e.*, to no purpose, broken; and a too vivid, a depressing, sense of mortality awakened within them,

> "Half conscious of their dying clay."

The high muse, Urania, reproaches the Poet for in this way arousing, in those who shared his loss, a fruitless grief, and thus counsels him:

> "Abide a little longer here,
> And thou shalt take a nobler leave."

Let him continue to cherish the past, with its keen sorrow, and it will be seen to have had wise and happy issues. And if he must at length leave it, and address himself to present and pressing duties, it will be in a worthier and nobler mood.

It should be observed, that those who divide In Memoriam into two parts only, (Azarias), make the second and victorious part, commence with this poem.

LIX.

Sorrow invoked as his life companion.

This beautiful poem was added in the fourth edition of In Memoriam, published in 1851. It forms a fitting sequel to lviii. The light in which sorrow is regarded, it will be noticed, is entirely changed from that in iii. and xxxix. The explanation of the change, as given by Genung, is "that Sorrow has fled from Nature to God, and in spite of Nature's evil dreams, can leave the problem of human destiny to Him, and can therefore be taken as a trustworthy guide." It means, at least, that he has begun to experience the benign influence of Sorrow, when rightly taken.

In accepting and even inviting her life-long companionship,—to live with him, "no casual mistress, but a wife,"—he counsels her, not to be always gloomy, but to "be sometimes lovely like a bride," if she will rule his life, and shape it to wise and good ends. He will not have her leave him, that cannot be; his "centred passion cannot move," but she must be with him in such fashion that

> "I'll have leave at times to play
> As with the creature of my love."

That must be in tuning his song to her gentler moods, and so tuning it, with such sprightliness of hope that the note of Sorrow will scarcely be recognized by others in his lay;

> "That, howsoe'er I know thee, some
> Could hardly tell what name were thine."

The whole poem is one of singular beauty and charm. There is a certain delicate and subtle witchery of fancy running through it, which it is difficult to define, but which it should not be difficult to recognize and to feel.

LX.

The misgivings of unequal love.

In this and in the five succeeding Cantos, the Poet deals with the relationship now subsisting between himself and his departed friend. That friend is contemplated, not as when he was yet on earth, " a soul " indeed " of nobler tone," but as still more ennobled, and in the same measure removed from his sympathy, by his entrance into a higher world. Their mutual relationship is now accordingly such, that he finds the image of himself in the village maiden who has set her affection on one of higher rank than her own, to whom, when he withdraws to his proper sphere, her native surroundings look poor and mean, and who, as she surveys them, " weeps " and says,

" . . . how vain am I !
How should he love a thing so low ? "

Like her, the Poet, too, doubts or despairs of the possibility of retaining his hold on the love of one, who has passed into a sphere so much above his own.

LXI

THESE MISGIVINGS SOMEWHAT ALLAYED BY THE CONSCIOUSNESS THAT HIS OWN LOVE ABIDES IN SPITE OF THE INEQUALITY.

This poem is closely connected with the foregoing, being as it were, its complement. Whereas in the former, the earthly life is viewed as mean and narrow by the Poet, in comparison with that into which his friend has passed, it is now his friend himself who so regards it, or rather who so regards the Poet in it. In his high estate, it may be his to hold converse with the greatest souls that have lived; with a Plato, a Dante, or an Isaiah: if so, "how dwarf'd and blanch'd," like plants deprived of warmth and sunlight, must his (the Poet's) growth appear. Notwithstanding let him turn his eye to the earthly shore, and he will find the love which is worth all else, in full vigor and himself its object.

> "I loved thee, Spirit, and love, nor can
> The soul of Shakespeare love thee more."

There is a kind of bold and violent self-assertion in these two lines, which seems out of harmony with the general tone of In Memoriam.

LXII.

THE SELF-ABNEGATION OF LOVE.

This poem attaches itself quite closely to the last. He is sure of his own love, and happy, as true love ever is, in its exercise. He has asked his friend to observe it from his high estate. The possibility is now contemplated, that this simple earthly love may be too unworthy to attract its object, may even make him "blench," start back, as at the sight of something unexpected and unwelcome, then let it be as "an idle tale," not to himself,—that it could never be,—but to its exalted object, to whose "deeper eyes" it becomes "matter for a flying smile," like some foolish early love, outlived in later years.

Thus what the Poem depicts at this point is the rare self-abnegation of which love is capable. It should be said, however, that this belongs only to love of the purest and loftiest sort. It is not all love which is content to give affection, without receiving it in turn.

LXIII.

YET SUCH SELF-ABNEGATION MAY NOT BE NECESSARY.

The higher being may feel affection for one much beneath him, and this without thereby being dragged downward. The Poet's own experience has taught him this. Man though he be, he can pity an overdriven horse, and give love to his dog, nor is he hindered in his upward aspirations by these feelings, of which dumb animals are the objects. So he, too, in turn, though so far beneath the friend who has been taken up into the life above, may be in his grief the object of his sympathy, without impeding him in his upward course.

> " So mayst thou watch me, where I weep,
> As unto vaster motions bound,
> The circuit of thine orbit round
> A higher height, a deeper deep."

The sentiment is simple and natural, and the expression strong, but the Canto scarcely rises either in the melody of the rhythm or in the tone of feeling to the general level of the Poem.

"In its assumption up to heaven," (1st stanza); in its heavenward aspirations; Dr. Gatty: "without robbing heaven of its dues of reverence."

LXIV.

The continued interest of his friend in the preceding earthly life and in himself as a part of it, suggested and sustained by another analogy.

This poem describes with a good deal of detail, and with much vividness and force, the upward career of a person of humble birth, but of lofty genius; his successful conflict with opposing circumstances, and his achievement in the end of the highest honors of the state, and then calls attention to the familiar and pleasing fact that there are moments in his life when the home of his childhood and the playmate of his youth rise to his memory with deep and tender interest. May not his friend, too, from the lofty height to which he has risen, feel an interest similarly strong and tender in him, his early mate?

The poem is a fascinating one. Its charm lies, not in the depth and intensity of the feeling expressed,—many surpass it in these respects,—but in its exceeding simplicity and naturalness. The fact which supplies the analogy is familiar enough, but it is wrought out with a singular combination of strength and beauty; so much so, that there are only few of the separate lyrics that supply a larger number of really striking lines.

Take the following :

"Who breaks his birth's invidious bar,"

"bar," *i.e.*, obstacle to success; "invidious," not in the sense of awakening envy, but in the sense of undesirable, offensive.

"And breasts the blows of circumstance,"

i.e., adverse circumstance.

"And grasps the skirts of happy chance,"

i.e., fortunate "chance."

"And grapples with his evil star,"

"evil" as having assigned to him a humble life.

"Who makes by force his merit known;"

"force," not here violence, but strength of character and of will.

"And lives to clutch the golden keys;"

"keys" as the well-known symbol of office.

"And shape the whisper of the throne;"

a truly felicitous phrase, one which has gone as a permanent expression into the language.

Then, when the Poet would depict the interest felt in moments of pensive memory by this "divinely gifted" and wondrously succsssful man in the scenes of his boyhood, it could scarcely be more touchingly expressed than in the words which represent him as feeling

> "A distant dearness in the hill,
> A secret sweetness in the stream."

LXV.

HE LIKEWISE MAY EVEN BE STILL SOMETHING TO HIS FRIEND.

This Canto may well be regarded as supplying the culminating thought in this cycle of the Poem, marking a great advance from lx. and lxii. In the happier mood which he has reached, he addresses the spirit of the departed in a tone of resignation :

> "Sweet soul, do with me as thou wilt."

He, on his part, soothes his troubled fancy with the thought of the imperishable constancy of love.

> "Love's too precious to be lost,
> A little grain shall not be spilt."

The love here may either be, his love to his

friend or his friend's love to him; it would seem to be best to regard it as inclusive of both.

Seized of this truth, the inspiring thought arises in his mind, comes fluttering up like a bird on the wing, and like that bird, self-poised, needing no support from without;

> "Since we deserved the name of friends
> And thine effect so lives in me,
> A part of mine may live in thee,
> And move thee on to noble ends."

This brief lyric has so many subtle turns of thought, that its beauty may easily escape the reader.

A series of poems now follows, in which the calmer mood reached by the Poet alternates as in lxxii. with the bitter, tumultuous feeling of loss. This series may be regarded as extending to lxxvii.

LXVI.

"IN THE MIDST OF UTTER DESOLATION THERE COMES A KINDLY CHEERFULNESS LIKE THAT OF THE BLIND."—F.W.R.

The Poet's gay moods excite surprise in one who had thought his heart to be diseased and warped by sorrow. In explanation he says that the loss he has met has not only not embittered him, it has touched his nature with kindly sympathies ;

> "Has made me kindly with my kind,"

like one who has lost his sight.

The picture of the simple and innocent pleasures of the man overtaken with blindness is wrought out with great beauty of detail and in language that any child can understand. We are made to see his helplessness rendering him sympathetic, his deprivation of higher satisfactions compensated by the greater pleasure which he feels in simpler and lower ones. As he indulges in these, he dreams of the sky he can no longer see. Then in two lines remarkable for their union of simplicity and force—lines full of pathos, which speak to the imagination and the heart, and cling to the memory, and which are equally applicable to the illustration and to the case which it is designed to illustrate—he gives us the whole light and shade of the situation ;

> "His inner day can never die,
> His night of loss is always there."

LXVII.

THE MOONLIGHT SENDS HIS THOUGHT TO THE TOMB OF HIS FRIEND, BUT NOW WITH A QUIETING INFLUENCE.

This is the first of a number of poems which present to us the action of the Poet's mind, in reference to his lost friend, during the night season, first in the waking and afterwards in the dreaming state.

In the poem before us, he is awake ; the moonlight, as it falls on his bed, sends his fancy to the marble tablet in Clevedon Church, erected in memory of his friend. He sees it illumined by the moon's "silver flame." The night advances ; "the mystic glory swims away." He falls asleep until the morning dawn, "till dusk is dipt in gray," and again he sees the marble whitening in the returning light.

The poem deserves, and will well repay careful study. It contains several felicitous expressions. The reader will notice the following : " closing eaves of wearied eyes," for falling asleep ; " dusk dipt in gray," for dawn ; " a lucid veil," that which hides the object on which it is cast, but is itself white and clear. The only expression which is at all difficult is, "mystic glory" as applied to the moonlight, the "silver flame" which steals slowly over the tablet. The meaning of the epithet here may be emblematical. The words "from coast to coast" must mean the coast from one side of the bay into which the Severn falls to that on the other, or from Somersetshire to Wales.

"In the dark church like a ghost," (4th stanza). In the earlier editions the line ran, "In the chancel like a ghost." The tablet, however, is not in the chancel of the church, as incorrectly stated in Mr. Hallam's private Memoir of his son.

LXVIII.

HIS OWN SADNESS TRANSFERRED IN THE DREAM-STATE TO THE FACE OF HIS FRIEND.

We have now the action of the Poet's mind in reference to his friend, during dreams, depicted in a succession of lyrics. It has been observed that in the earlier stage of his bereavement "clouds of nameless sorrow" darkened his dreams; now they are represented as calm and natural, though the sense of loss makes itself still felt amid them.

In the poem before us he represents himself as dreaming of his friend, the friend of whom

CANTO LXVIII. 137

his waking thoughts are full, but he cannot dream of him as dead.

"Sleep, Death's twin brother, knows not Death."

This will scarcely hold as a univeral truth. But in the Poet's case, if in dreams he calls up the form of his friend, he can only call it up as living ; he walks with him " as ere" *i.e.*, before he " walked forlorn,"

"When all our path was fresh with dew,
And all the bugle breezes blew
Reveillée to the breaking morn."

A fine description of the season of youth, made vivid by one metaphor after another ; the second being particularly striking.

Recalling his friend in dream, he sees a strange trouble in his face ; a trouble which remains unexplained while the dream lasts. He wakes early,

" . Ere the lark had left the lea,"

out of his vision-haunted sleep, to discover that it is the trouble of his own early and uncontrolled grief, which he has unwittingly transferred to the face of his friend. This is characterized by Davidson as " a fine piece of psychological observation."

"Times my breath," (1st stanza), referring to the fact that the breathing is slower and more regular in sleep.

LXIX.

HIS GRIEF, A CROWN OF THORNS, IS CHANGED INTO LEAF BY THE GLORY OF A HAND.

or

THE TRANFORMATION OF SORROW.

The dream continues or is repeated ; but the subject of the weird dream in this poem is not the lost friend, but the Poet himself. The dream, besides, is rather an allegory than a dream, or, at least, it is a dream which shaped itself into allegory. Nature, amid which he wanders, gives no sign of spring. Its ancient power is locked up in endless winter. The streets are blackened "with smoke and frost" and human speech is used only to chatter trifles. This is nature and human life as colored by his sorrow ; perhaps also, as viewed in the light of the barren scepticism of the age. A wood to which he wanders has no leafage even on which to rest his eye ; it has but thorny boughs, whereof he makes a wreath for his head. Wearing this, he becomes an object of merriment and scorn to those around.

> "They called me in the public squares
> The fool that wears a crown of thorns."

By this "crown of thorns" perhaps we may understand, not so much the piercing sense of loss under which he has suffered, as the songs, thus far so generally charged with pain and woe, in which he has given tuneful expression to it, and in words, too, that to many seemed exaggerated and unreal, and thus supplied material for merriment and scorn.

At this stage, an angel of the night, one of those celestial messengers whose task it is to deal with the darker experiences of life, "looked upon" his "crown and smiled," not the smile of contempt, but that of sympathy; also,

> " He reached the glory of a hand,
> That seemed to touch it into leaf."

This can only mean the transformation of his sorrow, and of his song with it, under some benign and heavenly influence which has reached him—"the divine thing in the gloom," which, we are told, the Poet meant by "the glory of a hand."

> " The voice was not the voice of grief,
> The words were hard to understand."

The Poet has told us, that even when he speaks in the first person, he is sometimes voicing not his personal feelings and experiences only, but the feelings and experiences of humanity at large, and which he shares in common with it. If we might regard him as so speaking here, then these words might be taken as pointing to the power, which belongs to the celestial ministry of the unseen, to transform the darker and more sorrowful experiences of life into the rich harvest of saintly character and undying hope. Compare 2 Cor., 4 : 17 ;—" Our light affliction . . . worketh a far more exceeding and eternal weight of glory while we look at . . . the things *which are not seen.*"

LXX.

Darkness. Futile effort to form a distinct picture of his friend.

The Poet makes the effort to recall at night-time the familiar features, striving to paint " on the gloom " the face he knows, but without success,

" . . . the lines are faint
And mix with hollow masks of night."

The state seems to be that between sleeping and waking, and while it lasts, those masks go on tumbling and mixing at their own will, a strange weird phantasmagoria;

> " Till all at once beyond the will
> I hear a wizard music roll,
> And thro' a lattice on the soul
> Looks thy fair face and makes it still."

As so often with the attempt to recall a word, or a name, the effort must cease in order to success, so in the present case, the familiar features of his vanished friend, resisting the effort of the active fancy to shape them into distinctness, come up spontaneously in a passive or quiescent state of will. But as this poem is found in the midst of a succession of dream-pieces, the state of quiescence, in which the else eluding image is caught, may in this case have to be thought as reached in sleep, and thus in that sense " beyond the will."

LXXI.

ONE SCENE IN THEIR PAST EXPERIENCE AT LAST VIVIDLY RECALLED IN DREAM.

The reference in this final lyric of the series is to a journey made by the two in 1830, through a district in " summer France." Sleep, which has often tortured him with fantastic visions, at last favors the Poet with one "night-long" vision of that tour, recalling

> " . . . the river's wooded reach,
> The fortress, and the mountain ridge,
> The cataract flashing from the bridge,
> The breaker breaking on the beach,"

these being the outstanding features in the landscape. This leads him to address sleep, as kin "to death and trance and madness," suspending like these the exercise of ordered thought and will. Having " such credit with the soul," such power to produce temporary illusion, it is invoked to "bring an opiate trebly strong," that no sense of wrong rising blindly may mar his pleasure as in the visions of the night, he talks as of old with his friend.

"The blindfold sense of wrong" may be supposed to refer, not to any wrong done himself in the withdrawal of a loved presence, but to Arthur's loss of the fame, which he must else have won, and to which explicit reference is made in lxxiii. Their talk was said to be "of men and minds," (the alliteration will be noticed, of which there are so many examples in the Poem, and to which, in part at least, its melody is due)," the dust of change." The expression is an obscure one. It does not necessarily stand in apposition to the clause which precedes, and may simply designate the Poet's sense of the light and trivial character of the objects and the interests which "change" was continually evolving; like "dust" they were blown hither and thither by every changing breeze. Once more, their talk embraced

" The days, that grow to something strange,"

the transformations wrought on private and social life, already so rapid in the Poet's day, and so marvellous.

LXXII.

First Anniversary of Arthur's Death.

This lyric, if there were no other evidence of the fact, would be enough to shew that the successive lyrics in In Memoriam were not written in the order of time, in which they stand in the Poem as a whole. Some allowance, no doubt, must be made for fluctuations in feeling, and for sudden outbursts of sorrow, even after a degree of calm has been reached. One of the Poet's commentators has found such a lapse here. The tumult of feeling in the lyric, however, is so great, the thought of the loss of which the day reminds him is so steeped in bitterness, that it is difficult to think its composition could have followed that of lyrics in some of which a sweet spirit of resignation has been seen.

The day, a day of September wind and rain, is graphically pictured as blowing "the poplar white" by the reversal of its leaves, as lashing "the streaming pane," and making the rose droop "with its quick tears," (a fine metaphor), and "the daisy close her crimson fringes;" with perhaps a subtle suggestion of resemblance to the day a year before—the day that for him

>   ". . . sicken'd every living bloom
>   And blurr'd the splendor of the sun,"

with evident reference to the power which belongs to a great bereavement, to change the whole aspect of nature to the mourner; "day" when his "crown'd estate," crown'd above all with such a friendship, "began to pine;" another metaphor of much beauty and force.

But so keen is his sense of loss, so rebellious his feeling, so completely is he taken possession of by it, that if, instead of rising in gloom and storm, it had been a day of peaceful sunshine or of gentle summer breeze, it would have looked

"As wan, as chill, as wild as now."

Addressing it, he bids it, as if laden "with some hideous crime," hasten to its joyless close, and "hide" its "shame beneath the ground."

One is reminded of Job's imprecation on the day of his birth. "Let the day perish on which I was born."

The feeling in the poem may well appear over-strained if not unreal; but given the feeling, the language in which it is expressed, and in which the aspects of nature are described, as seen through it, is wonderfully vivid and forceful.

LXXIII.

REGRET FOR THE LOSS OF FAME BY HIS FRIEND, MITIGATED BY THE CONSIDERATION OF ITS FADING CHARACTER, AND BY THAT OF THE INTELLECTUAL POWER WHICH WOULD HAVE ACHIEVED IT.

This poem and the four which follow are taken up with the subject of fame; first, his friend's, and then, as in some way connected with it, the Poet's own. The thought with which this first opens, is that of the multiplicity of interests in the universe, and of the greatness of the need which they involve.

> " So many worlds, so much to do,
> So little done, such things to be,"

He may not judge therefore by any narrow view of things, where, in what realm, his friend's powers were most needed or could be used to best advantage,

> " How know I what had need of thee,
> For thou wert strong as thou wert true ? "

But in any case, the fame on earth which he had anticipated for him, was not attained, nor to be attained:

> " The head hath miss'd an earthly wreath ! "

In this he finds ground for regret, but no longer for complaint. This, like all else, falls out according to unerring law; and besides, earthly fame has no endurance. "We pass." The place which knew us, knows us no more forever. The very path we trod is soon obliterated.

> " What fame is left for human deeds
> In endless age ? "

None.
> "   It rests with God.'

The meaning of the last statement therefore is not, as it seems to me, that it rests with God to determine what fame each shall have, but that God, that the Divine mind, keeps in perpetuity and that it alone keeps, the story of any heroic act or course of action. This is the solace to which he turns in view of his friend's head missing "an earthly wreath;" and this besides, the soul retains self-infolded the virtuous force, which with opportunity given, "would have forged a name." He therefore bids the "hollow wraith," the ghostly spectre, "of dying fame, fade wholly."

LXXIV.

His friend's kindred with the great comes out in death.

A fine use is made by the Poet in this lyric of a well-attested fact, that not infrequently a man's face in death reveals hitherto unperceived resemblances to some one of his race. Sir Thomas Browne, speaking of one recently dead, says, "He lost his own face, and looked like one of his near relations; for he maintained not his proper countenance, but looked like his uncle." In like manner, musing on his departed friend, he discovers his true character, his likeness to the wise and great of the race; but he does not see all, nor speak all he sees,

" . . . knowing Death has made
His darkness beautiful with Thee."

The thought and the expression in these closing lines of the poem are alike beautiful. One can hardly fail, however, to be struck with the contrast between the sentiment which they embody, and the bitter and rebellious feeling regarding the death of his friend pervading lxxii. Months, if not years, one would imagine, must have lain between the states of mind, which could find truthful expression in strains so wide apart.

LXXV.

THE FAME UNATTAINED HERE IS SURELY BEING ACHIEVED ELSEWHERE.

The opening stanza of this poem takes up the thought contained in the closing stanza of the last. In both stanzas there is reference to the same purposed silence regarding the merits of his friend; in the one, in these words,

> " But there is more than I can see,
> And what I see I leave unsaid,"

in the other, in these,

> " I leave thy praises unexpressed."

There is in point of fact thus far, not much of direct eulogy of his friend ; the same could not be said of the later poems. He is silent regarding his greatness, as feeling his incompetence to do it justice in his verse. He even shrinks from the attempt to do so, as if making an unworthy use of the qualities which had won his admiration and his love.

> " I care not in these fading days,"

days, in which impressions made are so soon obliterated,

> " To raise a cry that lasts not long,
> And round thee with the breeze of song,
> To stir a little dust of praise."

The skill and success with which the metaphor is carried out in these words, " the breeze of song, to stir a little dust," etc., will be observed. In any case, the world gives men credit for what they do, not for what they might or could have done ; but somewhere—beyond the veil—some high task is being "wrought with tumult of acclaim,"

"So here shall silence guard thy fame,"

which could only be injured by inadequate speech.

LXXVI.

THE FLEETINGNESS OF HUMAN FAME.

The transition from the fame, which, had life permitted, would have been Arthur's, to that of the Poet, who sings of his loss, is a simple and natural one. What immortality can the poet hope for his verse? Ascend in fancy to the zenith, look at the achievements of the modern poet from that high point, how do they not dwindle and disappear? Or pass in imagination into the distant future, "lighten," *i.e.*, take thy airy flight,

" . . . thro'
The secular abyss to come,"

and thou shalt see that "thy deepest lays" have ceased to charm, "are dumb," while the yew tree,[1] which saw their birth, is still green.

---

[1] The yew is selected as attaining to a great age; its life is numbered by centuries.

"The matin songs," the songs of Homer, of David may last, but thine shall wither before the oak has lived half its days.

> "And what are they when these (oaks) remain
> The ruined shells of hollow towers."

LXXVII.

IMMORTALITY FOR HIS VERSE HOPELESS, BUT HE WILL SING ALL THE SAME.

This is the last of what have been termed the Chorus poems. It need not detain us. It presents a view of modern song, which, however applicable to much of it, time thus far has happily shown to be inapplicable to the Poet's own; but even if applicable, if his verse, too, shall die, his

> " . . . . darkened ways
> Shall ring with music all the same."

To sing of his loss and of his love is sweeter to him than to earn immortality, even if by trying higher flights he might have hoped to do so.

LXXVIII.

ANOTHER CHRISTMAS. THE SENSE OF LOSS REMAINS, BUT NOW CALM AND NOT INCOMPATIBLE WITH MIRTH EVEN.

It is claimed by some that a new section of In Memoriam commences with this poem. According to Genung, it introduces a new Cycle, which he terms the Cycle of the Present, embracing lxxviii.–ciii. It is so designated because according to this writer, " the thought has to do with the present aspect of the Poet's love for the dead and of the immortal one's relation to him." The marking off of these twenty-five Cantos into a distinct section, with the above as its characteristic thought, seems to me very arbitrary. It has no obvious or even actual foundation in the contents of the included poems. If by " the present aspect of the Poet's love for the dead, and of the immortal one's relation to him," is meant " the aspect " at the time when the songs were written, then this is forthcoming in the earlier, as well as in the intermediate and later parts of In Memoriam ; while on the other hand, a poem such as lxxxvii. is wholly retrospective. The utmost

CANTO LXXVIII.   153

which can be said with certainty seems to be this, that the three successive Christmas poems indicate successive states of feeling, progress from utter unrelieved grief, through tranquil calm, towards hope and victory.

The change which has come over the Poem at this stage will be readily recognized, if we compare this Christmas celebration with the previous one (xxx.) Then the sorrow was tumultuous, like the storms raging without, and the observance of the Christmas usages was forced and cheerless ; now the sorrow is calm, as is the day with its hushed winds and its silent snow.

" No wing of wind the region swept ; "

a fine metaphor finely expressed.

But there is still "the quiet sense of something lost," brooding sleep-like over all things, it is so quiet, however, the Christmas observance proceeds with so much of ancient mirthful usage, that the Poet asks with startled feeling, "Can sorrow wane?" Is his grief for his friend actually lessened? That were worse than all!

"O last regret, regret can die!"

But no, his sorrow lives on within his " mystic "

being; "mystic," perhaps as able to combine strangely conflicting feelings, though tears are no longer shed.

"This is not victory," to quote from Stopford Brooke, "the grief is still only personal. The Poet has not escaped from himself, and the year which has been spent in half-intellectual analysis of doubts, and the replies of the understanding to them, has not brought peace to the life of his soul." Still from this point onwards "the change is towards recovery. Through the undertone of grief, there begins to flash up now and then, the note of hope, and gradually the hope grows stronger and more permanent, till at last the poem ends in hope so intense as to be almost joy. The recovery consists in the passing of grief unto hope, not in the passing of love into forgetfulness." (Tainsh).

LXXIX.

A FRIEND MORE THAN A BROTHER, AS SUPPLEMENTING DEFICIENCIES.

This poem is addressed to the Rev. Charles Tennyson, the Poet's brother, and at the time of its composition engaged to be married to

Miss Sellwood, a younger sister of Lady Tennyson. This circumstance may be—according to Dr. Gatty it is—the reference of the words in the first stanza; "the costliest love."

The tone of the poem is apologetic. The Poet has before him the line in ix. and quoted here,
> "More than my brothers are to me,"

and the fear is present to his mind that it may have hurt one who possessed the very strongest claims on his esteem and affection. He feels it his duty therefore to explain. The common influences, to which in childhood and youth they had been subjected, had moulded them alike; had made them both wealthy, but wealthy therefore with kindred qualities of mind and heart.
> "But he was rich where I was poor,
> And he supplied my want the more
> As his unlikeness fitted mine."

The brother is not the complement of the brother, as the happily chosen friend is. The picture of the way in which ancestry, nature in field wood and stream, and Christian training in the home, unite to mould the character and habits of an English youth, is drawn with great vividness and force, while it is one to captivate the reader by its naturalness and beauty. It could have been drawn only by one who had been reared amid the pure and healthful influences which it depicts.

"My wealth resembles thine," (5th stanza). It is a singular mistake which Dr. Gatty makes, in explaining these words by the fact, tnat each brother had in the two sisters a special and kindred object of affection.

LXXX.

HE FINDS HELP AND COMFORT IN THE THOUGHT OF WHAT HIS OWN DEATH WOULD HAVE BEEN TO HIS FRIEND.

This is one of four pictures of what might have been. The other three are lxxxi., lxxxiv. and xciii. In the present poem, the case is supposed, that he (the Poet) had died, and his friend had lived on. "Death," then, ("holy death," can scarcely be termed a felicitous expression), had

" . . . dropt the dust on tearless eyes,"

i.e., the Poet's eyes, which on this supposition had not known the sorrow of bereavement. His friend, on the other hand, would have mourned deeply but calmly, would have sorrowed but with the resignation that comes of trust in God and love to man; and the burden of sorrow thus borne would have turned to gain.

What better can he (the Poet) do, since he is the survivor, how more truly honor his friend, than bear his removal in the same sweet spirit of resignation, and with a like purpose to turn the burden of loss and sorrow into gain?

"His credit thus shall set me free,"

i.e., the noble yet gentle sorrow with which I credit him shall do so;

"And, influence rich—to sooth and save,
Unused example,"

unused because the alternative which was needed to allow the example to take effect was not realized,

". . . from the grave"
"Stretch out dead hands to comfort me."

It will add to the force of the last line if we take the word "comfort" in its old and proper sense of "strengthen."

LXXXI.

Love ripened by death.

We have in this poem, as in the former, another picture of "what might have been." But in this the supposition is, that he also had survived as well as his friend, and the point raised is, to what their mutual love might have grown! It must surely have ripened into an affection still sweeter and more mellow. "Love then" while he was still here

> " . . . had hope of richer store:
> What end is here to my complaint?"

The answer implied—that there is none—rather enlarges the room for regret. As he reflects on it, he hears "the haunting whisper" "which makes him faint,"

> "More years had made me love thee more."

To this Death gives the sweet reply:

> "My sudden frost was sudden gain,
> And gave all ripeness to the grain,
> It might have drawn from after-heat."

The allusion in these lines is to the effect of a

moderate degree of frost in hastening the process of ripening full-grown grain—grain nearly but not quite ripe. The illustration would not probably be regarded as so felicitous a one as most others employed by the Poet, in this region where "sudden frost" striking the unripe grain is so often "sudden" and great loss. Still, as applied to human life, it has undeniable truth. The recently formed, the immature and superficial affection, death terminates. The love, deeply seated, and based on character, death ripens and purifies, and that in brief time.

LXXXII.

But fellowship interrupted is the real bitterness.

A strong faith, one apparently unclouded by doubt, underlies this poem in the active and progressive life of his friend in another state of being.

" Eternal process moving on,
 From state to state the spirit walks."

Having this faith, death is not blamed because of the corruption to which it has subjected the object of his affection in " form and face ; " why mourn "the ruin'd chrysalis," which the spirit leaves as it moves from a lower to a higher state? Nor is it blamed, because it has deprived this world of a virtuous force which it needed.

> "I know transplanted human worth
> Will bloom to profit, otherwhere.

It is blamed, wrath against it rises within his breast, because it has made the delightful fellowshp of interchanging voices impossible between him and his friend.

"The divided nature and its complement" is said by Genung to be the subject of the last four poems, and much ingenuity is displayed in linking them together under this general heading. But the connections are artificial, and meanings are read into the songs at one point and another, which it is difficult to discover in the words, and not easy to believe were present to the Author's mind.

LXXXIII.

WINTER AND ITS DEPRESSION. SPRING LONGED FOR AS BRINGING INSPIRATION TO JOY AND SONG.

The season is that of the second New Year after Arthur's death. Comparing it with xxxviii., a song of the previous spring-tide, in which these words occur,

> "No joy the blowing season gives,
> The herald melodies of spring,"

we are made conscious at once of the changed mood. There is still sorrow, but it is a sorrow from which the Poet seeks to be released, not by forgetfulness of his loss, not by the narcotic of song, but by the influences flowing in on him from reviving nature. "His mood," Genung observes here with obvious right, "answers to the promise of the season and goes forth congenially to meet it." This change in the Poet's feeling, we may regard as due, partly to the healing influence of time, partly to his faith that "human worth," removed from earth, "will bloom to profit, otherwhere."

Impatient under the depressing influence of

winter with its suspended life, and eager for the return of reviving nature, he cries,

> "Dip down upon the northern shore,"

i.e., England as a northern region,

> "O sweet new year, delaying long;"

and again,

> "What stays thee from the clouded noon,"

i.e., of spring,

> "Thy sweetness from its proper place."

The lines which follow, and indeed the whole poem, bespeak the Poet's minute observation of nature in field and garden, his keen sympathy with it, and his sensitiveness to all its changing phases. It is as if the reviving life within him, needed the reviving life of Nature without, to set it completely free; and in his eager impatience, he cries once more, addressing now the New Year,

> "O thou, new year, delaying long,
> Delayest the sorrow in my blood,
> That longs to burst a frozen bud,
> And flood a fresher throat with song."

The metaphors in the last two lines are peculiarly beautiful.

LXXXIV.

THE HOME AND THE LIFE WHICH MIGHT HAVE BEEN.

This is the third of the four pictures of what might have been, had the life both of Arthur and the Poet been spared. As a picture of the domestic joy which must have followed his friend's marriage to his sister and of the career of usefulness and of honor, ending in a Christian's death, which his friend must have led, it is drawn with exquisite tenderness and warmth; drawn, as it could only have been by one to whom home with its tender and faithful love, its simple and pure joys, was peculiarly dear, and whose conception of civic life was singularly high and noble. In this respect as a revelation of the Poet, especially on the domestic side of his nature, it merits careful study.

It is unnecessary to enumerate all the details, which go to make up the picture, and which are drawn with so deft and loving a hand. We see the home to which his richly dower'd friend has led a loved sister of his own ; in that home this friend " crown'd with good " sheds happiness all around,

> "A central warmth diffusing bliss
> In glance and smile, and clasp and kiss."

Boys of his babble on their uncle's knee. In vivid fancy the Poet sees,

> " . . their unborn faces shine
> Beside the never-lighted fire."

No description could be more graphic. We see him, "an honor'd guest," in his sister's home, contributing his share to the genial and witty "table talk,"

> "Or deep dispute and graceful jest."

His friend meanwhile grows in power and "prosperous labor;" honors are heaped on him as the swift years pass on. At last their earthly courses finished and at one and the same moment, they reach together "the blessed goal," and are welcomed "as a single soul" by "the shining hand" of the Saviour.

All this might have been; but only seldom, if ever, is such a picture of domestic joy and prosperous labor, and blissful end, unmarr'd by loss or failure, permitted to become a reality In this case it was not:

> "But that remorseless iron hour
> Made cypress of her orange flower,
> Despair of hope and earth of thee."

To dream of it was to wake

> "The old bitterness again, and break
> The low beginnings of content."

It remains, nevertheless, an ideal to charm by its sweetness and purity, and to elevate by its noble and lofty spirit, the thousand readers of the Poem.

"Thy crescent" (1st stanza); properly applied to the moon on the increase, and so to Arthur's developing power.

"The dolorous strait" (10th stanza); that between the earthly and the heavenly life.

"Involved in thee" (10th stanza); their union unbroken even in death, or rather, in dying.

"Backward fancy" (12th stanza); fancy looking backward.

LXXXV.

HIS LOVE FOR THE DEPARTED COMPATIBLE WITH REAL BUT NOT WITH EQUAL LOVE FOR ANOTHER.

This poem is addressed, as might be gathered from a comparison of its second stanza, with the opening stanza of the Epithalamium, to one who was destined to sustain the same relation to the Poet as Arthur had been, and who thus became a candidate for the same place in his affection. We learn that this was E. L. Lushington, Professor of Greek in the University of Glasgow, who was about to be married to another sister.

The poem opens with the words, already found in xxvii., and repeats the sentiment there expressed, which we have seen to be the culminating achievement of the conflict with sorrow and loss at that point;

> "Tis better to have loved and lost,
> Than never to have loved at all."

The poem is in substance a lengthy reply to the question, supposed to have been put by this friend, as to the effect of his bereavement on his nature, on his trust in things above, and especially on his power to enter into new friendships. In the reply, there is none of "the old bitterness" which threatened to awake in the closing stanza of the preceding poem. The Poet has recovered again his hardly acquired calm; there is as much as ever of the old affection, but it is no longer permitted to betray him into an excess of grief. "I count it crime to mourn for any overmuch;" a marked change of feeling.

The reply is in narrative form. In not a few

of the stanzas we miss the simple Saxon words and sweet melody so characteristic of In Memoriam. The music, which pervades the Poem as a whole, is heard, however, in lines such as these, and not less the old intensity of feeling :

> "But summer on the steaming floods,
> And Spring that swells the narrow brooks,
> And Autumn, with a noise of rooks,
> That gather in the waning woods,
>
> And every pulse of wind and wave
> Recalls, in change of light or gloom,
> My old affection of the tomb,
> And my prime passion in the grave."

The reply goes back to Arthur's death; the manner of which is expressed in striking and memorable words,

> "God's finger touched him and he slept."

This death was followed by his friend's entrance on the blessed state, his own relinquishment,

> "To wander on a darkened earth,
> Where all things round me breathed of him."

But his grief has not unmanned him. He has found a reserve of strength even in the sorrow with which he has cherished the memory of Arthur,

>"An image *comforting*"

in the original and proper sense of, strengthening

>"the mind,
>And in my grief a strength reserved."

His "imaginative woe," moreover, that is, his woe bringing his imagination into play, in handling the great questions which death raises regarding the destiny of the spirit, "diffused the shock" of bereavement "through all" the life, and thus broke the violence of the blow at the moment of its occurrence. He is ready to form other friendships, all the more ready that this one is now beyond the destroying power of time ; nay, that the spirit of him who was its object, as it speaks within him, or "yearns to speak," counsels some new attachment. Accordingly, he woos the love of the new friend, and assures him of his own true love, though love not equal to that which he had felt for the departed ;

>"If not so fresh, with love as true,
>I clasping brother hands, aver
>I could not, if I would, transfer
>The whole I felt for him to you."

CANTO LXXXV.

He offers him therefore,

> " The primrose of the later year,
> As not unlike to that of spring."

The two stanzas commencing, " And I, Can clouds of nature stain," etc., raise a question, on the supposition of any knowledge possessed by the departed of the state of those on earth, very old and of very great interest. The answer,

> " I triumph in conclusive bliss
> And that serene result of all."

does not aid us much in understanding, how the bliss of heaven to those enjoying it is consistent with their knowledge of the subjection to pain and in many cases enslavement to evil, of those dear to them on earth.

" Thro' light reproaches," etc., (4th stanza). Something like reproach was implied in the interrogations mentioned ; but if implied, it was only half expressed and it was loyal to the law of kindness.

" Equal-poised control," (9th stanza) ; a quality said to have been very characteristic of Arthur.

" Other form," as disembodied.

" Whatever way my days *decline*," (11th stanza) ; with reference to the course of life as moving steadily downward.

" For which be they that *hold apart*," (27th stanza), *i.e.,,* that hold " the promise of the golden hours," in ways all their own—with peculiar firmness.

LXXXVI.

SUMMONS TO NATURE, NOW IN THE BLOOM OF SPRING TO COME TO THE RELIEF OF HIS STRICKEN SPIRIT.

This poem attaches itself very easily and naturally to the last stanza of the preceding one. The call to Nature in her Spring freshness and beauty to shed her balmiest influences on him may well be connected with his proffer of a new friendship. It is impossible not to be struck with the depth and intensity of the sympathy with Nature—"the gorgeous bloom of evening" in the western heavens, the sweet and gentle breeze sweeping across the meadow, and "shadowing down" the stream "in ripples,"—a sympathy itself the sign of returning health to his affections—which is here revealed.

The poem, it will be observed, forms one long sentence. In it he entreats the "ambrosial air," "ambrosial"—delicious, as the air often is after a shower; "slowly breathing bare" *i.e.*, making bare of clouds: "the round of space," and streaming thro' "the dewy-tassell'd wood," and down the darkly-rippling brook, to fan his brows and "blow the fever from" his cheek,

CANTO LXXXVI. 171

and infuse "the full new life that feeds" its breath, "till Doubt and Death, ill brethren, let the fancy," the imagination, fly

> " To where in yonder orient star
> A hundred spirits whisper ' Peace.' "

This poem betrays in almost every line the close and minute observation of Nature which is everywhere conspicuous in his poetry. Tennyson rarely interprets nature as does Wordsworth, but he describes it truthfully and vividly, and he sets it, as here, in close relation to his own changing feelings. Commenting on the poem before us, Stopford Brooke says: "Each verse is linked like bell to bell in a chime to the verse before it, swelling as they go from thought to thought, and finally rising from the landscape of earth to the landscape of infinite space. Can anything be more impassioned and yet more solemn? It has the swiftness of youth and the nobleness of manhood's sacred joy."

"And shadowing down *the horned flood,*" (2nd stanza). The reference is to the water as curling over the intercepting rocks and horned in its motion like the young moon.

" And *sigh* the full new life," (3rd stanza) : that is, impart as by a breath or sigh.

LXXXVII.

RECOLLECTIONS OF COLLEGE LIFE AND FRIENDSHIP.

Cambridge is revisited, whether in fact or in fancy, is not just apparent. It lives and must ever live in the memory of the Poet, as the place where his friendship with Arthur was formed, and as the scene of the larger part of their intercourse. His altered feeling at this stage is seen in the circumstance that there is no trace any longer of passionate grief in his description of the once familiar scenes, but rather a kind of melancholy pleasure in surveying them ; such as we feel in renewing acquaintance with any scene, that recalls vividly the face of a lost but still cherished friend. The city, its halls of learning and its churches, the river and the "gray flats," the rows of limes and of willows, come successively before us. We hear "the storm" of the pealing organ, "the measured pulse of racing oars," and the "noise of songs and clapping hands." But the mind is taken back to the Cambridge of the Poet's youth and early friendships, to its Society in which

"... once we held debate, a band
Of youthful friends, on mind and art,
And labor, and the changing mart,
And all the framework of the land,"

and of which Arthur is ever the central figure, "the master-bowman" ever cleaving the mark, the eloquent speaker, with face lit and form lifted by "the rapt oration," on his brow the stamp of intellectual power.

"The bar of Michael Angelo."

"The *high-built* organs" (2nd stanza); probably as reared above the screen, which separates the choir from the nave.

"A band of youthful friends" (6th stanza); the Society to which the Poet and his friend belonged, and called "The Apostles," embraced Trench, afterwards Archbishop of Dublin, F. Maurice, and Arthur Phelps, among others; but according to another account, said by Mr. Knowles to be that of the Poet himself, the reference is to the "Water Club," so called because there was no wine used.

"The God within him" (9th stanza); with evident allusion to the Martyr Stephen.

"The bar of Michael Angelo" (10th stanza); the great painter, we are told, had a strong bar of bone over his eyes.

LXXXVIII.

UNACCOUNTABLE EXTREMES OF FEELING MEET IN HIS HEART AND PULSATE IN HIS SONG.

In this brief but intense lyric, the nightingale is addressed, popularly regarded as commingling joy and grief in her song. Like her, the

Poet feels himself driven between fierce extremes of feeling. He bids her unfold "the secret of that tumultuous passion of song," which is now full of grief and now again of rapture. Sorrow should preponderate in his song; that was what might be expected,

" And I—my harp would prelude woe—"

but no, his passion, too, has in its midmost heart a secret joy. The order and harmony of the universe makes itself felt within his breast.

"The glory of the sum of things
Will flash along the chords and go."

The mind of the Poet, it will be observed, is at this stage no longer restricted to his personal loss. He sees himself to be but a part, a minute fractional part, of the whole of being; a whole which, despite his personal griefs, is harmonized by love and justice. The order and glory of the universe begin to dominate his grief.

The depth of passionate feeling, weighted with noble thought, which is reflected in this brief, but really exquisite poem, will not be overlooked. The passion is no longer the bitter one of personal loss. " The sweetness of memory and the soothingness of faith have discharged bitterness from the soul," (Stopford Brooke), but the intensity is as great as ever.

LXXXIX.

RECOLLECTIONS OF ARTHUR AT SOMERSBY.

Somersby in Lincolnshire was the Poet's birthplace and early home, to which Arthur had made more than one visit. He is thus led to give us a series of pictures of the country life of a simple but refined and cultured English family. The present is the first of the series. Another follows in xcv.

As we read the poem, we are made to see the changing light and shade on the green lawn, to feel "immantled in ambrosial dark" the cool retreat of the over-arching elms, and from it to watch

"The landscape winking through the heat,"

to hear the swift measured stroke of the scythe in the grass, and the sudden gust of wind among the pear trees; to listen to Arthur's voice, as he reads his favorite Tuscan poets, or discusses with his friend "the books to love and hate," or rails against "the busy town," and to that of the sister, happy in her lover, as she flings

"A ballad to the brightening moon."

Nor are other sounds, still oftener heard in rural life, wanting. The milk bubbling in the pail, the bees buzzing in the air, mingle with the flow of mirthful jest and grave discourse. The pleasures of nature and of art, of intellect and of taste, unite to form as noble and charming a picture of simple country life as has ever been drawn. Happy is the land that can supply such scenes, and that had, too, a poet who could depict them with pen at once so sympathetic and so skilful. And now "something of the calm and bliss" of those fast retreating days steals over the Poet as he lives them over again in his song.

"Witch elms .... towering sycamore" (1st stanza). This last is again referred to in xcv. ; we are told it is now cut down, and the four poplars are also gone and the lawn is no longer a flat one.

"Winking through the heat" (4th stanza); an extremely felicitous and expressive metaphor.

"The bounding hill" (8th stanza); the hill which bounded their view at the Rectory.

"Before the crimson-circled star, etc." (12th stanza); that is, before the planet Venus had sunk into the sea, the grave of the sun. According to La Place's theory, this planet is evolved from the sun.

XC.

WHERE LOVE IS TRUEST, THE PLACE OF THE LOST IS NEVER FILLED.

The Poet, who likes to play now with one fancy, now with another, "making them vassal unto Love," in this poem deals with the fancy of his friend's return to earth. The disconcerting effect which a return to life would in many cases have, gives him the opportunity for that use of contrast, of which he is so fond. In the case of the heir, who had entered on the possession of another's estate, in the case of the bride, who had given her hand to another suitor, the reappearance of the former owner, or the former lover, must needs awaken mingled feelings, might even work "confusion worse than death." But for Arthur, on his part, there would be no "iron welcome,"

> " . . . but come thou back to me :
> Whatever change the years have wrought,
> I find not yet one lonely thought,
> That cries against my wish for thee."

The possibility of this utter fidelity of love, a love weighted with thought, and based on character, is that which ennobles human existence.

He, who doubts its possibility, the possibility of a love which masters time, and to which the sense of loss never dies, has

> ". tasted love with half his mind,
> Nor ever drank the inviolate spring
> Where nighest heaven."

"Yea, though their sons were none of these" (5th stanza); "none of these," that is, none of the class before mentioned, hard heirs, or those who had married others' brides.

XCI.

The desire for his friend's return associated with the reviving life of spring, and with the brightness of warm summer sunbeams.

This poem, it will be noticed, attaches itself easily and naturally to the former, and carries forward its thought. The indignant disclaimer, with which that poem closed, passes over in this one into an eager cry of longing; " Come." Come, with the glory of either season; spring-like,

> " The hope of unaccomplish'd years
> Be large and lucid round thy brow,"

i.e., the promise of great achievements, which, thy early death did not suffer to be realized, be lucidly visible on thy forehead, or summer-like,

" . . . beauteous in thine after form,
And like a finer light in light."

Nothing is to our senses purer than light. The imagination of the Poet soars above sense, and on its wings he sees his friend return, "like a *finer* light in light."

This is an exquisite picture, first of spring, then of summer, executed in each case by a single touch or two. In spring, we see the fresh rosy tufts of the larch, and the deeper blue of the kingfisher, we hear the exquisite notes of the thrush; in summer, we have the sweet fragrance of the rose, the ripple of the waving wheat field and the warm sunbeam brooding over all. It is our Poet's way of depicting nature, whether in her summer calm or in her winter storm, to make use of one or two bold touches, not, as is the method of some other poets, of lengthened descriptions.

XCII.

YET SUCH RETURN NO LONGER TO BE EXPECTED.

We have in this poem a striking contrast to xiv. The states of feeling portrayed in each are as widely remote as possible. Then the

Poet would have felt nothing strange in the return of his friend, unaltered in look and mien, " no hint of change in all his frame." Now the certainty of separation has become fixed. Were the vision granted, which in the preceding poem he desired, did his friend return to him, either " with the hope of unaccomplished years on his brow," or with the summer-light of glory wreathing his head, would he be able to believe that it was really he?

> " I might but say, I hear a wind
> Of memory murmuring the past."

Yea, though the strange presence should shew minute acquaintance with the past, in which their " lots were cast together," or make predictions, verified by the revolving year, would he not have to count it an illusion, the work of a distempered brain, an objectifying of his own presentiments or memories?

> " . such refraction of events
> As often rises ere they rise."

"Refraction of events" (4th stanza). The reference here is to the scientific fact, that the sun, by refraction, still appears in full size above the horizon, after it has really sunk below it, and reappears in full, when only just the upper edge has reached the horizon. (Dr. Gatty).

Note.—This and the two preceding poems appear to afford conclusive evidence that Genung is not warranted in assigning the meaning to this part of In Memoriam which he does. His heading of the poems xc.-xcv. is, "In his peace with all bereaved, he finds communion in spirit with the dead."

XCIII.

But his very self may come in spiritual form.

No approach discoverable by the senses is to be expected. The burden of the preceding poem was, an approach of this kind, even if made, would not be credited. The opening statement in this one is, it is not to be looked for. "I shall not *see* thee." But the spirit itself may come, spirit to spirit, by methods of approach unknown to sense, may come through channels

> "Where all the nerve of sense is numb;"

can take no note whatever. In an appeal full of passion, the Poet pleads

> "That in this blindness of the frame,"

this inability of the bodily senses to detect a spiritual presence,

> "My Ghost may *feel* that thine is near."

What is desired here is obviously something more than, something different from, communion with the departed as generally understood by us. By this we usually understand, a vivid sense of their persons, their nearness or their presence to imagination and thought and feeling, implying rather our approach to them, than theirs to us; a change in our feeling rather than in anything external to us. The Poet seems to have contemplated something more than this as possible, and not as possible only, but as actually realized by him.

"I therefore from thy sightless range" (3rd stanza); "range," that is, which cannot be observed by sight; thus, not without sight but beyond sight.

"Unconjectured bliss" (3rd stanza); *i.e.*, bliss great beyond conjecture, with a reference probably to 1 Corinthians 2:9, "Eye hath not seen, nor ear heard, neither have entered into the heart of man, the things which God hath prepared for them that love Him."

"Of tenfold complicated change" (3rd stanza); such as the spirits of the departed may be supposed to undergo in the higher sphere of being, into which they are regarded as having passed.

XCIV.

THIS APPROACH TO BE EXPECTED BY THOSE ONLY WHOSE HEARTS ARE PURE AND CALM.

There are spiritual conditions which must be forthcoming, the Poet tells us, if spirit is to meet spirit, that is, to meet good spirit, for of such only is he speaking. Spiritual communion presupposes spiritual affinity, some degree of resemblance to those with whom communion is sought. They have done with all discord and passion; with such thou, too, must have done, if thou would'st know and feel them near.

> " They haunt the silence of the breast,
> Imaginations calm and fair,
> The memory like a cloudless air,
> The conscience as a sea at rest : "

> " But when the heart is full of din,
> And doubt beside the portal waits,
> They can but listen at the gates,
> And hear the household jar within."

The poem is from first to last an eminently truthful and an exquisitely beautiful picture of the moral state, the state of heart and life, which conditions all highest communion, the communion, not less, with the uncreated spirit. Every line is marked by its own beauty.

XCV.

THE SPIRITUAL COMMUNION REALIZED IN A STATE OF ECSTASY.

This poem, one of the most striking in In Memoriam, opens with a fine picture of a summer evening in the country. All nature is still, save as its silence is broken by the gentle murmur of the distant brook, and the sweet voice of song. Trees stretch "their dark arms about the field," while kine couch at ease on the neighboring knolls, and moths flit through the dusk "with ermine capes and woolly breasts and beaded eyes." The whole peace and loveliness of the scene seem to steal in upon us, as we read the lines which describe it.

Evening passes over into night. One after another of the company withdraws, and the Poet is left alone. "A hunger" seizes his heart. We may regard this as meaning a keen desire to have closer fellowship with the living spirit of the departed than any yet realized. In this mood of ardent longing, he takes out some of his friend's letters, which are finely described as

"Those fallen leaves which kept their green."

"The silent-speaking words" of the letters are picturesquely represented as strangely breaking on the silence of the night, and as strangely answered by "love's dumb cry." The bold and vigorous faith of the writer courageously facing doubt rises before him as he reads, and in what must be regarded as a waking trance or state of ecstasy,

CANTO XCV.

"The dead man touch'd me from the past,
And all at once it seem'd at last
The living soul was flash'd on mine,

And mine in his was wound,"

with this result, he was whirl'd aloft,

"and came on that which is,"

that is, on real being as distinguished from the merely phenomenal existence apprehended by the senses. In this state, the movements of the world, "the shocks of Chance, the blows of Death," often to us in our ordinary moments so full of disharmony are heard by him as sweetly musical ;

"Æonian music measuring out
The steps of time."

It is difficult to know in what light exactly we are to regard this experience of the Poet, for an actual experience it seems to have been, which the lines record. The Poet himself seems to have been somewhat at a loss regarding it, as is evident from an important change made on the original form of the poem at this point. Instead of the words now found in the last line of the ninth stanza, and the first of the tenth, the first edition had these:

"*His* living soul was flashed in mine,
And mine in *his* was wound."

Evidently the Poet shrunk on reflection from the claim implied in these words. "His conscience," we are told, "was troubled by the '*his*'" found in these lines. The change to "*the* living soul," if an improvement in one respect, does not in another fit in very well with the context. On the whole, the words employed imply a sense of the presence of the departed of a more direct and close kind than is reached either by memory or imagination simply. The state in which he found himself on reaching it, may be compared to that ecstasy described by Thomas Aquinas and the Mystics generally, to that of Dante with his famous vision, if not even to that of St. Paul, 2 Cor. xii. Tennyson, as has been already said, was on his own shewing remarkably susceptible of such abnormal conditions.

At length the trance, which continued till dawn,

"Was cancell'd, stricken through with doubt,"

the result of the return of sense and intellect or understanding.

The poem closes with a picture of the dawn, unsurpassed in poetic beauty by anything found in In Memoriam. The last three lines are specially beautiful in the subtle resemblance which they disclose ;

> " And East and West, without a breath,
> Mixt their dim lights, like life and death,
> To broaden into boundless day."

"In matter-moulded forms of speech," (12th stanza); referring to the familiar fact, that our words, expressive of spiritual ideas, are borrowed from words primarily denoting sensible experiences.

XCVI.

The doubt, that leads to stronger faith, defended.

This is the first of a series of poems, not consecutive, in which the Poet gives us, what has been termed, "part portraitures" of his friend; for there can be little doubt that he is the person referred to in the poem before us.

The picture, one drawn to relieve the feeling of some gentle and pious woman, perhaps his sister, that all doubt of religious truth is "devil-born," is that of a person who had doubted, but who had fought his doubts and laid them, as distinguished from others, who also have to confess to the presence of doubts, but who simply turn away from them as wicked, or at least as destructive of their peace, if not also of their goodness. In the earliest stage, that of awakening thought, there was in Hallam's case, as in that of so many, mental discord. He

> " . . touched a jarring lyre at first,
> But ever strove to make it true;
> Perplext in faith but pure in deeds,
> At last he beat his music out."

Thus the duty of the hour, as the Poet defines it, when faith in the spiritual verities is shaken, and doubt is in the ascendant for the moment, is to do the right, to keep the conscience clean, and to face, instead of running away from "the spectres of the mind." It has to be said, that the firmest and most inspiring faith in divine realities is often reached in this way. The truth for which a man has had to wrestle with doubt, when once recovered, is usually both better understood and more prized, than if no such doubt had ever arisen. The possibility of doubt is involved in the circumstance that the object of faith is insusceptible either of logical proof or of sensible verification. The value of it, or the absence of value, depends altogether on the character of the doubt, and the spirit in which it is dealt with. It is certainly not to be regarded as in itself a good.

The lines follow, so often quoted, not always

wisely, nor in the sense in which we may believe the Poet wrote them:

> "There lives more faith in honest doubt,
> Believe me, than in half the creeds."

The term "creeds" is here used, not its ordinary and proper meaning, that of systems of belief or doctrine, but in the sense of the beliefs which are cherished by men in these systems, the mental assent which they give to them. The truth in the statement, so far as it contains truth, is somewhat to this effect, that a man honestly doubting, not denying but simply doubting, and wrestling with his doubt, not cherishing it, may have more real faith, that is, a profounder sense of the reality of the unseen and eternal, than one who gives an unthinking assent to the fullest creed ever formulated.

The victory of the man who "fought his doubts and gathered strength" is expressed in these striking lines,

> "And Power was with him in the night,
> Which makes the darkness and the light,
> And dwells not in the light alone."

The reference would seem to be to God, whose presence and benign operation — hence the name used here, Power, for the Divine Being—

is regarded as at work in the darkness as in the light, in the doubt which is struggling onward to faith, as in the faith which has laid hold of the unseen.

XCVII.

His relation to Arthur in his exalted state compared to that subsisting between a married pair of unequal attainments.

The first stanza of this poem is somewhat mystical. The main truth implied would seem to be that the heart dominated by love gives its own color to all in nature and in human life by which it is surrounded, projects itself into every object which meets its view.

"He sees himself in all he sees,"

even "as the giant-spectre sometimes seen 'on misty mountain ground' is no more than the vast shadow of the spectator himself." In the present case it is an unequal marriage, but one in which the early love remained undiminished by the inequality, which is made to prefigure the existing relationship between himself and his friend; we say existing, for we are expressly told by the Poet himself, that what he "would describe is the relation of one on earth, to one in the other and higher world," not his own relation to his friend here.

Towards his friend, who now lives "in vastness and mystery," he feels as a wife might feel towards a husband, with whom there was formed in the days long ago a union of real affection, but from whom high pursuits, in which she can have no share, now separate her. Meantime "her life is lone," but not either loveless or cheerless. She looks now and again at the old love-tokens;

> "She keeps the gifts of years before,
> A wither'd violet is her bliss."

She does not doubt that the love which bestowed it is still cherished towards her, though it is no longer given her to taste its sweetness as once. It is the greatness to which he has grown, greatness which she cannot even understand, that separates him from her.

> "For that, for all, she loves him more."

It is not assuredly an ideal union of man and woman, but perhaps just because of this, it all the more aptly pictures the Poet's relation to the friend whom death has in a manner transfigured.

The comparison, it must be said, is wrought out with great beauty of detail, and with a simplicity, which apparently artless, is really the perfection of art. The alternations of light and shade, of real love and of seeming coldness, in the picture of the simple-hearted wife are peculiarly striking, *e.g.*,

> " He loves her yet, she will not weep ;
> He seems so near, and yet so far,
> He looks so cold ; she thinks him kind."

The state of mind which the Poet has reached in relation to his departed friend is finely mirrored in the closing stanza,

> " Her faith is fix'd and cannot move,
> She darkly feels him great and wise,
> She dwells on him with faithful eyes,
> ' I cannot understand ; I love.' "

XCVIII.

VIENNA, WITH ALL ITS BEAUTY, TO HIM DISMAL.

A friend is going to Vienna, where Arthur had died. This is enough to rouse anew the sense of loss and to invest the city, in itself so beautiful, with forbidding qualities of the most marked character. It is known how capriciously the mind acts in circumstances of the

CANTO XCVIII.

kind, how the place associated with a friend's death will sometimes gain a new charm in consequence, sometimes become an object of aversion. Vienna acts on the Poet in the latter way. Its splendor, which his friend had often celebrated, is of the deceptive kind;

> "No livelier than the wisp that gleams
> On Lethe in the eyes of Death."

Then in language extremely strong and vivid, evil is represented as haunting the city and dogging the steps of its inhabitants from the cradle to the tomb;

> "A treble darkness, Evil haunts
> The birth, the bridal; friend from friend
> Is oftener parted, fathers bend
> Above more graves."

The very "blaze of kings" is shadowed to his fancy by the everywhere prevailing sadness.

The pervading sentiment of the poem, the keen and bitter sense of loss which it expresses, would be strange and not easily accounted for, if the separate poems which constitute In Memoriam had been written in the order in which they stand in the collection.

"Summer belts of wheat and wine," (1st stanza); these belts are the marked features in the landscape in a great part of Germany.

"Each cold hearth," (5th stanza); cold, either as uncheered by the open fire, or, as without domestic love.

"Any mother town," (6th stanza); English rendering of metropolis.

XCIX.

ANOTHER ANNIVERSARY OF ARTHUR'S DEATH—
ALL ARE KIN TO THE POET, TO WHOM IT
BRINGS LIKE MEMORIES OF LOSS.

It is natural to compare this poem with that written on the previous anniversary. It opens with the same words,

"Risest thou thus, dim dawn again."

There is still the same sense of loss,

"Day when I lost the flower of men;"

but the tumult of rebellious feeling is no longer heard, nor nature moaning as if in sympathy therewith. The grief has become calm and nature with it. Her breath is balmy. The winds no longer howl, "issuing out of night." They murmur in the foliaged eaves—a beautiful figure—

"A song that slights the coming care."

The sounds which meet the ear are not "blasts which blow the poplar white," "and lash with storm the streaming pane," but "voices of the birds" and "lowings of the herds." But the greatest change observable is, that the sorrow which the day renews is now touched with sympathy towards all, to whom it brings as to him, not memories of bridal or of birth, but memories of death.

> " O, wheresoever those may be,
> Betwixt the slumber of the poles,
> To-day they count as kindred souls ;
> They know me not, but mourn with me."

This last circumstance has been taken for all it is worth by Genung and others as evidence of the escape from a merely personal sorrow ; perhaps for more than it is worth. Genung says, " the sorrow there (on the previous anniversary) renewed was centred in self, while this sorrow is touched with sympathy for all who have similar sad memories." But fully to justify this statement, would the Poet not needed to have written " I mourn with them," instead of they " mourn with me ? "

" Betwixt the slumber of the poles," (5th stanza) ; that is, over the whole earth. "The poles" are the imaginary ends of the axis on which the earth revolves ; they remain at rest, "slumber" while other parts move.

C.

EACH FEATURE OF THE LANDSCAPE WHICH HE IS ABOUT TO LEAVE RECALLS HIS FRIEND, AND LEAVING IT, THAT FRIEND SEEMS TO DIE ANEW.

We have in this poem another beautiful sketch, the details of which are filled in with all the deftness of the Poet's art. The occasion is his leaving Somersby, the home of his childhood and early youth. The scene, which is in Lincolnshire, is largely pastoral. The golden waves of the wheat field, "the long arms" of the spreading elm, and the broad river, are not here. In their place we have the "lonely fold," the "low morass," the "simple stile," the trilling linnet, the "wrangling daw," the "runlet tinkling from the rock;" all picturesque details of a pastoral landscape. It is a scene from which he is about to pass, and which accordingly once more recalls the friend who had in other days enjoyed its simple and healthful charms in company with him. Of these details which go to make up the landscape, he says,

> " Each has pleased a kindred eye,
> And each reflects a kindlier day ;
> And, leaving these, to pass away,
> I think once more—he seems to die."

CI.

THE LANDSCAPE LOSES THE EYES TO WHICH ITS VARYING FEATURES ARE DEAR AND SACRED.

In this simple and sweet poem, the Poet in prospect of change of residence, laments that tree flower and brook will no longer have the eyes which had watched their changes with fond delight.

" Unloved, that beech will gather brown,
This maple burn itself away ; "

referring to the fact that the beech becomes brown, the maple red under the autumn sun. Unloved, the rose-carnation, too, will

" . . . . feed
With summer spice the humming air ; "

in which the bees are at work.

Uncared for, the brook will babble

" At noon, or when the lesser wain,"

the Ursa Minor, or Little Bear, a small constellation, containing the Pole Star, and which in England never disappears,

" Is twisting round the polar star ; "

"Or into silver arrows break
The sailing moon in creek and cove;"

referring to the fact that the moon's reflection in the brook, as it runs along, becomes broken into silver arrows. Compare xlix., stanza 1.

All this will continue until, in the course of years, new associations gather round flower and brook, and other eyes come to regard them with delight.

The poem, like so many others, bears testimony to Tennyson's close observation of and intense sympathy with Nature in its changing aspects. In it, and the preceding poem, we have conspicuous examples of landscape "humanized by tender feeling," so much so that it seems half-conscious of the mingling emotions of delight and regret with which it is regarded.

CII.

His heart clings to the old home, bound to it by two feelings which in the end melt into one of pure regret.

The hour for leaving the Rectory, in which the Poet was born and in which mother and children have lived after the father's death, has come. A last ramble is taken through the grounds. He is made conscious of a two-fold spell, which the place throws over him. It is the home of his childhood, of his earliest and most innocent, if not of his highest, joys.

> " . . Here thy boyhood sung
> Long since its matin-song, and heard
> The low love-language of the bird
> In native hazels tassel-hung."

But it is also the scene of former delightful companionship with Arthur—

> " . . . Yea, but here
> Thy feet have strayed in after hours
> With thy lost friend among the bowers."

Does this circumstance invest it with a still dearer and more sacred interest? He may not say; but as he turns to go, the two feelings, which the leave-taking of the place awakens

> " . . mix in one another's arms
> To one pure image of regret."

"Gird the windy grove," (4th stanza); that is, "gird" in the sense of surround, with "the brook" as the subject of the verb.

"Lops the glades," (6th stanza); trims the hedges or thickets.

CIII.

ALL THAT HAS SERVED HIM IN HONORING HIS FRIEND WILL ACCOMPANY HIM INTO THE LIFE BEYOND.

This poem presents not a little difficulty to the interpreter of In Memoriam. Such questions as these arise: Does the poem record an actual dream, accompanied by the vision which it describes with its changing scenes? Or, is it an allegory in the form of a dream? Whether the one or the other, are all the details to be regarded as significant, or, as so often in the case of the parable, have we to be content with the one leading thought, the numerous details having significance only as the necessary appropriate setting of that thought? We incline to the view that what we have here is a simple allegory, possibly suggested by some dream of the Poet before leaving the residence in which he had lived with his maiden sisters, certainly borrowing some of its coloring from the nature of his surroundings there, that we are therefore not to regard all the details as significant, and that the main thought in the allegory is, according to the Poet's own interpretation, as given by Dr.

Gatty, that "the Muses, Arts," etc., "the maidens" of the story, "everything that has made life beautiful here," are to be carried over into the life beyond. The voyage of the poem, therefore, is not to be thought of as his going from one place of residence to another, but as his passage down the stream of being, and that not so much in his individual capacity as representing the human race.

The general meaning of the poem is thus plain. The maidens who dwell with him in the hall are not his sisters, not at least in their personal character, but poetry, art, music, science, etc.; all that has contributed to enrich or adorn life. The veiled figure of his friend, his memory, had brought all these—shall we say—poetic, artistic, and scientific endowments of the writer into exercise.

" . . in the centre stood
A statue veiled, to which they sang;"

" . . then flew in a dove
And brought a summons from the sea."

These words are significant. According to Brother Azarias they mean, "he feels called to other life-duties than those of weaving songs around the memory of his friend. He must proceed to fulfil those duties. The maidens weep lest they should now be neglected; but they accompany him." And they not only accompany him down the stream of existence, they gather "strength and grace and presence, lordlier than before;" and he himself feels clothed with new power, as his muses poured out new songs.

> "As one would sing the death of war,
>   And one would chant the history
>   Of that great race which is to be,
> And one the shaping of a star."

At length the voyage nears its end. The Here gives intimations of passing into the Hereafter. The maidens, the muses, arts, etc., fear they are to be left behind, and set up a wail. But their fear is groundless. They, too, pass into the life beyond.

The poem, of which this seems the main scope, receives only added significance and force, when the allegory is viewed as representing the experience of the human race, rather than that of the individual poet. The last lines are peculiarly striking, having all the mystery of eternity stamped upon them;

> "And while the wind began to sweep
>   A music out of sheet and shroud,
>   We steer'd her toward a crimson cloud
> That landlike slept along the deep."

Genung regards a new Cycle, what he terms the Cycle of the Future, as commencing at the point in In Memoriam which we now reach. He claims it to be distinguished from the two Cycles which are said to have preceded this, in that the future of which it sings is " no longer confined to a single new friendship, but takes in the whole race of man ;" and the friend whose loss the Poet has mourned in the earlier parts, " is connected with this greater future by being taken as its type." In accordance with this, poems cix.—cxiv. delineate his high qualities. This would appear to be a large induction from the facts before us. It may be conceded, however, that it contains an element of truth. There is certainly an advance in the feeling from this point; there is less of personal sorrow, more of wide, catholic, human love.

CIV.

CHRISTMAS EVE UNDER NEW ASSOCIATIONS.

The Poet is now in his new home, which, we are told, was at High Beach, Epping Forest; and the church mentioned is Waltham Abbey Church. The first two lines are identical with those describing the first Christmas Eve after Arthur's death (xxviii). But instead of "four voices of four hamlets round," it is

> " A single peal of bells below,
>   That wakens at the hour of rest,
>   A single murmur in the breast."

The murmur is one of regret, that while the season recurs, all the old associations are broken; the very bells sound "like strangers' voices;" "not a memory strays," *i.e.*, wanders amid the scenes within the reach of their peal;

> "But all is new unhallow'd ground;"

"ground," that is, without any of those tender associations which had lent ineffaceable sacredness to the scenes he had left behind.

CV.

THE OLD CHRISTMAS CUSTOMS UNSUITABLE IN THE NEW CIRCUMSTANCES.

The return of Christmas is not now to be marked by the holly being hung upon the wall. This were out of keeping with the "father's dust left alone and silent under other snows." That tribute, formerly paid to Use and Wont, can be well dispensed with in the new abode.

Grief shall no longer be made to assume the mask of gladness.

> " For change of place, like growth of time
> Has broke the bond of dying use."

Still the petty cares of life are to be thrown off and the mind be left free to quiet, thoughtful brooding on the past; but nothing further, no bowl, no song, no dance,

> " For who would keep an ancient form
> Thro' which the spirit breathes no more ? "

In other words, the old observances are to be dropped because the associations which lent them propriety and charm, have been broken. This is something very different from that for which, with the view of sustaining a certain theory in regard to the Poem, Genung pleads. He says, " The usual customs have lost their life, because the *spirit* of Christmas hope has become so settled and significant that the ancient form can no more express its meaning. The cheer of this season not only eclipses the grief, but rejects all formal demonstrations of joy as unnecessary and meaningless." Any careful student can see that a good deal has to be left out of the poem, and not a little read into it, to make it bear such a meaning.

"... No motion, save alone
What lightens in the lucid east

Of rising worlds by yonder wood."

This "refers," to give Tennyson's own words as found in Dr. Gatty's book, "to the scintillation of the stars rising." The Poet, moreover, has in his eye a good age, an age of triumphant goodness, as before the race. Its coming lingers;

"Long sleeps the summer in the seed."

The summer is viewed here as the seed, or the seed-time of the autumn. In his impatience, he bids it, or, perhaps, "the rising worlds" "run out," their "measured arcs, and lead," that is, usher in,

"The closing cycle rich in good."

CVI.

The new year; its bells summoned to ring in the era of triumphant good.

This is one of the poems through which the Poet has sought to become, and has in good measure become the prophet of his age. He lets us see his ideal, in respect both of that which he desires should pass away, and of that which he desires should come in. This ideal, as we see at a glance, is intensely moral, and it is very lofty. It is embraced, moreover, with a passionate eagerness, and with a noble scorn, which makes itself felt in every stanza, of the things in individual and social life opposed to it.

He will have the bells which ring out the dying year and ring in the new, ring out falseness, class feuds, party strife, faithless coldness, spite and slander, "the narrowing lust of gold," even

> "The grief that saps the mind
> For those that fiere we see no more."

ring in truth, redress of wrong, sweeter manners, purer laws, the common love of good, the larger heart, the kindlier hand,

> "the Christ that is to be,"

not here the personal Christ, though Dr. Gatty so takes it, but the humanity, the race, worthy to bear his name. The whole poem is pervaded by a noble vein of sentiment, and by aspirations of the very loftiest character.

CVII.

ANNIVERSARY OF ARTHUR'S DEATH, NOW CELEBRATED WITH MUSIC AND SONG.

The spirit of the Poet is entirely changed, since this season, the year before, when he spoke of the day as one "marked as with some hideous crime," but nature is not in sympathy with his new and happier mood. It has put on a wintry fierceness. This furnishes the Poet with the opportunity to give us one of his very finest pictures of a wild winter night. The sun goes down early,

> "Behind a purple-frosty bank
> Of vapor, leaving night forlorn."

The wind blows fiercely from the north-east, "and bristles," that is, makes erect, "all the brakes and thorns to yon hard crescent." We see the long pointed icicle hanging from the eaves, the frosted branches on brake and thorn gleaming in the moonlight. We hear the leafless limbs rubbing one against the other, and clanging in the breeze. Again we observe the storm leaving the land, to sweep over the

sea, its white drifts darkening as they meet
" on the rolling brine."

By one or two vivid touches, the fierceness of
the storm and its wild, wide sweep are brought
before us. The very words, full of rough, hissing sounds, seem charged with the rage of the
storm which they describe.

But it is Arthur's birthday, and the Poet
will have it kept with honors. The new mood
within overcomes the depressing influences
without. The logs shall blaze, the wine shall
flow, the cheerful talk proceed,

" . . . with festal cheer,
With books and music, surely we
Will drink to him, whate'er he be,
And sing the songs he loved to hear."

So changed is now the whole mood,

CVIII.

SYMPATHY WITH ONE'S KIND NECESSARY TO RIPEN THE FRUIT OF SORROW.

A tendency of sorrow, often seen, is to isolate
the person who experiences it. We have all
witnessed the self-absorption of a great grief,
and closely connected with this, is its tendency
to make its subject indifferent or even insensible

to the sufferings of others. Has the Poet yielded too much to this tendency since his great bereavement? This poem seems to betray something like a consciousness of this on his part. At least he will yield to the tendency no longer;

> "I will not eat my heart alone."

He will not in selfish isolation brood on his grief, and thus "eat" his "heart," consume its sympathetic power;

> "Nor feed with sighs a passing wind;"

add to the "passing wind" a breath of sighs; very vivid and realistic.

> "What profit lies in barren faith,
> And vacant yearning?"

Such a question makes one feel that the reaction from his brooding sorrow and soaring speculation has gone almost too far. Why should faith be barren or yearning vacant? No genuine faith, no healthful spiritual longings are fruitless, or fruitful in anything but good. Still his solitary brooding is not healthful, even if it seems to lift him in thought to the heights of heaven above, or carry him down to the mysterious depths below, to which death conducts.

He seems to say in the third stanza, that thus musing, it is after all but the shadow of himself, the reflection of his own qualities, which is pictured to his fancy.

> "What find I in the highest place,
> But mine own phantom, chanting hymns?
> And on the depths of death there swims
> The reflex of a human face."

There is probably a deep and important truth implied in these lines. It is difficult, indeed, to reconcile the view which they present with much that he has said; for has he not seen and professed to show us one much nobler than himself? But then the poet is not required to be consistent; he is the creature of moods. This is especially true of In Memoriam.

In human sympathy, then, and in human fellowship, he will seek the fruit of wisdom which sorrow is said to yield. It will be noticed that the fruit of sorrow, of which he speaks, is not that which we are so often accustomed to associate therewith—purity, gentleness, goodness; it is *wisdom*, wisdom as distinct from knowledge. Of this, more in the poems which follow.

CIX.

"What he was."—(F.W.R.)

It has been noticed that there is little of eulogy in the earlier part of In Memoriam, so little that considering the design of the Poem— to form a shrine for his friend—its absence, or at least its very limited presence, can hardly fail to strike us. In the latter part, it is entirely different. In xcvi. we have already had one sketch of Arthur ; now we have five following in succession. The first is an appreciative rehearsal of his intellectual and moral qualities. It looks, indeed, as if it were the Poet's intention to portray a part of that wisdom, which in the last line of the preceding poem, he had spoken of as sleeping with his friend.

In the poem before us, there is a fine blending of the intellectual and the moral in the excellence depicted ; power of rich discourse acquired in an intellectual home, refined and discriminating taste,

> "The critic clearness of an eye,
> That saw thro' all the Muses' walk."

"Seraphic intellect" at the command not of

doubt, but of truth ; a faculty of reasoning that readily glowed with the fire of passion ; the love of goodness, but no asceticism ; the love of freedom, but no hysterics ; the glow of youthful passion, but pure as snow ; all the grace of woman, united to the strength of man ; a face to win the confidence of childhood,

> " . . . the child would twine
> A trustful hand, unask'd, in thine
> And find his comfort in thy face ;"

Did such excellences as these meet in the friend over whom the grave had closed, but whom it had been his privilege to know, then, if he has not learned much,

> " My shame is greater who remain,
> Nor let thy wisdom make me wise."

CX.

THE INFLUENCE OF HIS PERSONALITY ON OTHERS.

So richly dowered, the charm of his presence was magical ; young and old alike felt it, " the men of rathe," that is, early, " and of riper years." It strengthened the weak,

> " The feeble soul, a haunt of fears,
> Forgot his weakness in thy sight."

It softened the severe, and shamed the false or the foolish. In the Poet it kindled admiration and "passionate love, and the emulation, too, that is born of love."

The poem is an exquisite word-picture of a rare and lovely character. Its charm is due in part to the effective use of antithesis, of which we have a fine example in the last stanza;

> "Nor mine the sweetness or the skill,
> But mine the love that will not tire."

This charm grows on us with every line, till in the end we reach the warm, almost reverent affection with which its original was regarded by the Poet, an affection which we admire, but at which we can no longer be surprised. It seems a species of violence to subject a work of art so perfect to any analytical process. The main thing is to look at it steadily till its beauty takes possession of us.

"The feeble soul, a haunt of fears" (1st stanza); are unusually felicitous expressions.

"To flicker with the double tongue" (2nd stanza); with some reference to the serpent's tongue. The word was "treble" in the original edition.

CXI.

HIS GENTLE HEART.

The churl may be seen in all ranks, even in the kingly—in " him who grasps " the " golden ball " of state—the rude nature breaking out in unguarded moments, through fashion's veiling forms, here termed "the gilded pale," that is, boundary or fence ;

" For who can always act ? "

that is, play a part which does not belong to him. But Arthur had that nobility of nature which no unguarded moment could surprise into ungentle words or acts. Gentle of heart, he was all that others seem, and " best seemed the thing he was." In his case, no .even passing spite narrowed or darkened the eye,

" Where God and nature met in light ; "

the reference probably being to the love or gentleness of God, and the grace or beauty of nature.

" And thus he bore without abuse
 The grand old name of gentleman,
 Defamed by every charlatan,
And soiled with all ignoble use."

The poem is a sweet and gracious picture of a character itself gracious and beautiful.

CXII.

The reserve of power in him.

The Poet is chidden by some one, in that, while tolerant of marked defects, he shews slight appreciation of narrower merit in those around him—the merit or "perfectness" of persons more scantily endowed. "High wisdom," wisdom, that is, that counts itself high, thinks him at fault in this. His defence or his explanation is, that he is so possessed by his friend's excellence, not narrow or bounded, rather boundless, that he is able to feel little interest in inferior souls, "the lesser lords of doom," as he terms them. "Lords of doom" even they are, as having through their possession of free-will the destiny of a life at their disposal, nay, in a measure, of other lives as well as their own; "lesser lords," as less largely dowered with intellectual power.

And that in his friend, which drew his special admiration was the reserve of power which ever belonged to him; so that one knew not what to expect, or, rather, what not to expect;

> " Hope could never hope too much,
> In watching thee from hour to hour."

What was seen as this marvellous power was exerted, was order evolved out of confusion, and calm out of storm,

> " And world-wide fluctuation sway'd
> In vassal tides that followed thought ; "

that is, large and fluctuating movements or tides of feeling followed obediently his thought, became vassals thereto.

This impression of a reserve of power, which a certain class of mind makes on the observer, is, it may be remarked, an unmistakable index of intellectual greatness.

CXIII.
THE PUBLIC LOSS SUSTAINED BY HIS DEATH.

We have here another poem which has for its subject, "What might have been." The poem opens with the repetition of the line from a former lyric.

> " 'Tis held that sorrow makes us wise."

Here, however, the statement is but the background for the thought of the wisdom that sleeps with his friend, wisdom that would have greatly served the public need in the years to come. The conception of the age in which his lot is cast present to the Poet's mind, is that of one of stormy unrest and startling change ; the whole fabric of religious thought and social life agitated

> "With thousand shocks that come and go,"

an age full of eager enthusiasm, but full likewise of danger. What might not one so highly endowed, at once so wise and so firm, have been to it! Not only "a pillar steadfast in the storm," but, when the time was ripe for the change, a power to give a new and higher direction to thought and life ;

> "A lever to uplift the earth
> And roll it in another course."

CXIV.

Wisdom inclusive of reverence and charity preferable to knowledge.—Both met in Arthur.

We have here one of the most important poems in In Memoriam, so far as making us acquainted with the thought of Tennyson on the great problems of life. It lacks the exquisite beauty and the musical rhythm of many of the poems. Several of the stanzas, indeed, are far from musical; for our Poet they are rough and broken. But what the piece lacks in smoothness, it gains in force. The Poet becomes here again the prophet, and puts his readers on their guard against the loud pretensions of knowledge.

There is, however, no indiscriminate abuse of knowledge; on the contrary, the poem opens with a warm commendation of her, such as comes fittingly from the pen of one who was more deeply interested in the advancing science of the time than any English poet of his age. By "knowledge" we are to understand that acquaintance with the universe, its facts and its laws, with man and with nature, which comes through the senses and the understanding; that to which he has reference in the Prologue, when he says :—" We have but faith, we cannot know, for knowledge is of things we see." Tennyson, as has been said, was himself an enthusiastic lover of knowledge, and so says,

> "Who shall rail
> Against her beauty? May she mix
> With men and prosper! Who shall fix
> Her pillars?"

that must be, so as to stop her progress. "Let her work prevail."

But like a half-grown youth, vain of his powers, but knowing neither what their limits are, nor how to guide them, she is reckless, and

> " Leaps into the future chance,
> Submitting all things to desire ; "

that is, she is governed by feeling, by passion, knowing nothing of restraint or self-control. Her insufficiency to be man's guide in life is seen in this ; she has no consoling assurance to give regarding the Hereafter;

> " She cannot fight the fear of death."

Cut off from love and faith, she is not only weak, but like some Minerva, sprung "from the brain," not of Jupiter, but " of demons ; " she is dangerous, animated by a wild, unloving lust of power. Knowledge must not lead, must be content to walk side by side with wisdom, like the younger child,

> " For she is earthly of the mind,
> But Wisdom heavenly of the soul."

The distinction is not exactly that of intellect and emotion or feeling, though it is not far from it. The "mind" as here used is that in man which deals with the facts and laws of the phenomenal world ; the " soul " that in him which is the seat of faith and reverence and charity. His friend, from whom his thought is never allowed to travel far, or travels at all, only to bring from its journey some new tribute to his worth, is the type in his eye of one who had learned the secret of keeping knowledge and wisdom in happy partnership.

> " I would the great world grew like thee,
> Who grewest not alone in power
> And knowledge, but by year and hour
> In reverence and charity."

CXV.

THE POET'S FEELING ANSWERING TO THE REVIVING LIFE OF SPRING.

We have in this poem one of the most charming pictures of spring which English poetry supplies. It is introduced not, of course, for its own sake, but for the purpose of being set in a certain relation to the Poet's own feeling. Different views may be taken as to what that relation exactly is. According to Tainsh, " the poem strikes the keynote of the remainder of this spiritual history. The summer of former happiness is over and gone, the winter of sadness and mourning is past; life reawakens in the world, and the glorious summer once more lies before. Regret is dead, or is changed to hope. The words of Stopford Brooke, who ordinarily interprets the Poet with much wise discrimination, are to the same purport. "And then last of all in the spring of 1836, (cxv., cxvi.) regret has wholly died. The re-orient life of the world is the symbol of the departure of the wintry grief that looks back to a friendship which seemed lost, and symbol also of the gain of the new friendship that is to be." But it is more than doubtful whether it was the intention of the poem to set the past and the future in the exact relation to each other which these interpretations of it imply. It is not doubted that the *bitterness* of sorrow or regret is represented as over, when the Poet wrote the lyric, but one may well doubt whether he meant to signalize the death of regret and the birth of hope, in saying,

" . . . my regret
Becomes an April violet
And buds and blossoms like the rest."

Rather the Poet represents himself in these lines as in full sympathy with the reviving life of nature, and finds therefore the regretful sense of loss which had been dormant for a time, reviving likewise within his breast. This is the view of the poem taken by Genung and Mrs. Chapman.

The various effects of spring, in earth, sea and sky, as these appeal to the eye and to the ear ; the fresh green of the hedge, the bloom of the violet, the song of the lark, the flocks whitening the fields, the milky sails floating in the breeze on stream and sea, are given with striking beauty. All these " wake answering chords in the Poet's breast." The last stanza comes on us with one of those surprises of tender feeling, of which so many are found in In Memorian. The lines have been already quoted. They furnish a fine example of the blending of external nature and human feeling, which is one of the well-known characteristics of our Poet.

" Now fades the last long streak of snow" (1st stanza); " streak," often the form which the snow assumes just ere it disappears.

"Now burgeons every maze of quick" (2nd stanza); " burgeons." buds or sprouts. " Every maze, etc.;" thickly intertwined plants.

"The lark becomes a sightless song " (2nd stanza); the beauty of the expression will be noticed.

CXVI.

Regret and hope mingle; hope preponderates.

The scope and contents of this poem are given very fairly by Davidson in these words : " Blossoming regret " is not the only flower in the spring-garden of the Poet's heart. Faith and hope blossom too. The music, stir and life of spring

> " Cry through the sense to hearten trust
> In that which made the world so fair."

The Poet's sympathy with nature is such, that the reviving life of spring stirs feeling within him, the feeling of regret, first of all (cxv.) ; but that is not the only feeling, not even the strongest ; " Not all regret." If out of the past, the loved face still looks, and the loved voice still speaks, that look, and that voice now awaken less of regret, more of hope ; the "bond that is to be " is more eagerly desired than the severance that has been is regretted.

> " Yet less of sorrow lives in me,
> For days of happy commune dead ;
> Less yearning for the friendship fled,
> Than some strong bond which is to be."

"The crescent prime," (1st stanza); the growing first part of the year.

"Still speak to me of me and mine," (2nd stanza); that is, of his sister as well as of himself.

CXVII.

**PRESENT SEPARATION WILL ONLY ENHANCE THE
DELIGHT OF REUNION.**

In this brief poem but a poem charged with intense feeling, the very separation which has been so touchingly mourned, is viewed with a kind of thankful rapture, as tending to intensify the desire for reunion, now regarded as certain, and to enhance its "delight a hundredfold." when it shall be realized. The lapse of time is even viewed as having this happy result for its end ; that lapse, whether measured by the sandglass, or the sun-dial, by the clock on the wall, or the sun in the heavens.

"Delight a hundredfold accrue,

For every grain of sand that runs,
And every span of shade that steals,
And every kiss of toothed wheels,
And all the courses of the suns."

CXVIII.

THE CHANGES THROUGH WHICH THE EARTH HAS PASSED FROM CHAOS TO HUMAN LIFE CARRY IN THEM THE ASSURANCE, OR THE HOPE OF PROLONGED EXISTENCE AND CONTINUOUS PROGRESS FOR THE INDIVIDUAL AND FOR THE RACE.

Nature as contemplated formerly lv., lvi., was charged with suggestions of despair in regard to immortality; as viewed now it is pregnant with hope, alike for the race and the individual. The successive stages through which, as science teaches, this planet has passed, "the solid earth" arising from a sea of fire, and undergoing one change after another, until at length man appeared, the crown, thus far, of nature— all this continuous progress from lower to higher—suggests the thought of a like progress uninterrupted by death, for man. This analogy between nature in her ever-upward progress, and man, is viewed in the poem in a twofold connection; first in relation to the departed, awakening the trust,

CANTO CXVIII. 227

> " . . . that those we call the dead
> Are breathers of an ampler day
> For ever nobler ends."

and second, in relation to the living man, who is summoned to arise and "type this work of time within himself from more to more," and thus to become

> " The herald of a higher race,
> And of himself in higher place."

The agonies of nature, realized in fire and flood, are to find their counterpart in man, moving forward and upward,

> " Crowned with attributes of woe
> Like glories."

The reference in these words, is no doubt, to the place which belongs to suffering in furthering this upward movement. The figure of ore purified by fire, and afterwards wrought into articles of strength and beauty, is then employed to illustrate the process by which character is transformed and moulded, and is carried through with a skill and a felicity of conception and expression, unsurpassed by any other passage in the Poem. Man crowned as above is to show,

"That life is not as idle ore,

  But iron dug from central gloom,
    And heated hot with burning fears,
    And dipt in baths of hissing tears,
  And battered with the shocks of doom

To shape and use."

The ore is purified and moulded by forces external to itself; man in part at least by a force within. He is summoned therefore to

    " . . . Arise and fly
  The reeling Faun, the sensual feast;
  Move upward, working out the beast,
  And let the ape and tiger die."

The lower nature, that which betrays a certain kinship with the beast, is to be subdued; the higher, that which shows its kinship with God, is to become ascendant.

CXIX.

THE HOME OF ARTHUR NOW REVISITED WITHOUT GRIEF.

This brief poem follows the former very naturally. With the assurance reached that his friend has entered on an unending and ever-advancing life, with the regret of severance retiring in presence of the hope of reunion, he can revisit, whether in fancy or in fact, Arthur's old home, not now with pain (compare vii.), but with delight,

> " . . . not as one that weeps
> I come once more."

It is early morning. The quiet of the city is still unbroken; save by the chirp of birds and the stray wagon, loaded with the sweet-smelling hay and suggesting the summer meadow. Within his breast, too, there is the calm of sweet and grateful memories, and the summer of sunny hopes. In this new and happier mood, he can say as his friend rises to his imagination,

> "And in my thoughts with scarce a sigh
> I take the pressure of thine hand."

CXX.

Renewed assertion of his confidence in the hereafter.

The words with which this brief poem opens —" I trust I have not wasted breath "—show us the importance which the Poet attached to his work, as a vindication of a future life. This is seen, too, in the last lines of the stanza:

" . . . not in vain
Like Paul with beasts, I fought with death."[1]

These lines are entirely misunderstood by Genung, as is indeed the whole force of this brief poem. The fight is by him supposed to be "a fight of faith with death," and such a fight, it is said, "proves man infinitely more than any mere materialistic therory can explain." That may be true, or it may not; it is not what is expressed in the lines. What the Poet will express is the confidence, or at least the hope, that the arguments he has adduced in favor of a future life are not of no account— that his fight with death at one point and another in the course of his work has not been vain. He thinks he has conquered death. To understand this claim, which the lines quoted, advance, it is only necessary to remember that death is only, and in the full sense of the word, death, when it is viewed as terminating man's personal existence.

The Poet's hope of immortality rests on his belief that the materialistic view of man is

---

1. See 1 Cor. 15: 32.

baseless; or at least an opposite view of man's nature is indispensable to his hope and is what gives life all its value.

> "I think we are not wholly brain,
>   Magnetic mockeries;"

"mockeries," that is because we imagine ourselves to be something more and higher than on that supposition we really are.

If science could disprove the possession of a spiritual nature by man, if the Poet could believe that man was "wholly brain," that thought in him was a mere function of nerve-fibres, then, indeed, his hope of any life beyond would vanish, and with its disappearance, his interest in science and in all else here.

> " . . . I would not stay."

All that gives nobility to life has in that case gone.

The last stanza, "Let him, the wiser man who springs hereafter, etc.," is spoken ironically. The whole poem is a protest against materialism, but, as Tennyson himself says, as quoted by Dr. Gatty, "not against evolution." The consistency of this distinction will depend on the sense in which the term "evolution" is employed. When in the last line he says, "But I was *born* to other things," the force would seem to be, that he finds himself possessed by nature of an instinct, which is irreconcilably opposed to a materialist view of man.

CXXI.

"HESPER - PHOSPHOR. — GRIEF HAS SLOWLY CHANGED ITS MOOD, AS THE EVENING STAR PASSES INTO THE MORNING STAR."—F.W.R.

This has been pronounced to be the most finished poem of conscious art in In Memoriam. It supplies another example of the skill with which the Poet makes use of Nature to reflect his changing and changed feelings. Phosphor, the Morning Star, heralding the sun's rise,

"Behind thee comes the greater light;"

and looking down on the awakening life of the world, is identical with Hesper, the Evening Star, which had watched the sun descend beneath the wave, and the active life of man go to sleep; it is the same planet Venus, however widely contrasted the aspects of human life are as seen by it, in the evening and in the dawn.

He, too, like that planet, is unchanged. "His love is there, and his loneliness, and the 'deep relations' of his grief are ever the same" (Mrs. Chapman), but his experience has altered. The gloom of evening becoming "ever dim and dimmer," has passed from the world to his eye, and the brightness of morning has arisen on it.

> "Sweet Hesper-Phosphor, double name
> For what is one, the first, the last,
> Thou, like my present and my past,
> Thy place is changed; thou art the same."

The conception is not an original one with the Poet, it is found already in Greek poetry, but the detail with which it is wrought out, the delineation by a few vivid touches of the opening and the closing day, is equally simple and beautiful.

CXXII.

Reminiscence of and longing for blessedness of the ecstatic kind.

The reference in the first stanza may either be to the experience described in xcv., where he says "The living soul was flashed on mine, and mine in his was wound," or, more generally, to the period when he was still struggling with rebellious feeling, and his sky was darkened by the sense of irreparable loss—" while I rose up against my doom "—the loss of his friend, "and yearned to burst the folded gloom ;" the gloom composed of many folds and thus thick. The former reference seems the more probable. On this supposition we must regard him as here recalling the occasion, when his soul was in some way so brought into contact with "the living soul," as to be lifted above the gloom which lay on it, as to have his creative imagination called into play, and to be made to feel the essential and eternal order and harmony which prevail. He yearns to have the experience renewed, to have his friend

" . Enter in at breast and brow,"

that is at heart and head, at the seat of feeling and the seat of thought, and thus through the inspiring presence, "as in the former flash of joy"—the occasion when on reading the letters of his friend, he was transported into a state of ecstasy—he longs to "slip the thoughts of life and death," and rise on the wings of fancy into the realms of pure being. In this state of ecstatic gladness,

"All the breeze of fancy blows

i.e., blooms,

> And every dew-drop paints a bow,
> The wizard lightnings deeply glow,
> And every thought breaks out a rose."

This will be the happy result of the re-entrance of his friend into his life, into his thought and feeling, now that he is no longer rebellious with his doom, and no longer under the thick gloom of grief. All nature will put on brightness and beauty to his eye.

CXXIII.

LOVE ABIDES AND THE SPIRIT IN WHICH IT DWELLS, AMID ALL THE CHANGES OF THE MATERIAL UNIVERSE.

The Poet reverts again to the startling changes which the material universe is ever undergoing. Some of these are graphically pictured; the deep rolls where the tree grew; the rush and roar of traffic is heard, where once the depths of ocean lay in their unbroken stillness; the granite hills change their forms, and "the solid lands melt like mist," or come and go like clouds. What hope of permanence there either for love or for the spirit which cherishes it?

None, and the time was (lv., lvi.), when the sight of all this state of flux, this disintegration of the most solid objects of nature, alarmed him, threatened to quench the hope of immortality within his breast. Now, as a spiritual being he contemplates it unmoved.

> "But in my spirit will I dwell,
> And dream my dream, and hold it true;
> For though my lips may breathe adieu,
> I cannot think the thing farewell."

This brief poem is a very important one, in the light which it throws on the situation to which the Poet came in the end. The presence in him of a spiritual nature of which he is directly conscious, and the spiritual affections of which that nature is capable, forbid to him the idea of extinction of being in death. Amid all change which we witness, amid all change even which we experience, there is one thing fixed and abiding, that which we call spirit. In this abiding principle, therefore, he will "dwell and dream" his "dream;" that must be, his dream of reunion with the departed; "and hold it true." Having such a nature, extinction of personal being, eternal separation from the object of affection is unthinkable.

> "I cannot think the thing farewell."

CXXIV.

The Heart asserts God in face of the Doubt of the Sense and of the Intellect.

The consciousness of a spiritual nature, and the belief in immortality, are very closely connected with belief in a supreme creating and controlling power, that is, in God. The poem before us deals with this belief; a belief which when attained is "our dearest faith;" when shaken "our ghastliest doubt." This

> "Power in darkness whom we guess,"

is not discoverable by the sense, nor is He capable of apprehension by the understanding. Intellect and sense are alike inadequate to give us God, to assure us of His existence or to determine His character;

> "I found Him not in world or sun,
>   Or eagle's wing, or insect's eye,
>   Nor thro' the questions men may try,
> The petty cobwebs we have spun."

But if amid this helplessness of sense and of intellect to give him God, the Poet was at any time disposed to entertain the thought of a Godless world;

> "Heard an ever-breaking shore
> That tumbled in the Godless deep;"

the heart within would rise in revolt, and exclaim, "I have felt." We are not told what exactly the feeling was, which asserted itself in face of the doubt of the intellect, and ultimately triumphed over that doubt. Perhaps the Poet himself would have had difficulty in defining it. It may have been the keen, unmistakable, and inextinguishable sense of the incompleteness of life without God, or, that sense of the infinite which is borne in upon the soul betimes; Mrs. Chapman terms it, "the perennial need of the universal human heart."

> "No, like a child in doubt and fear;"

This "No" is the protest of the heart or of the spiritual nature against the denials of the sense or the understanding; coming short, indeed, of resolving difficulties, but important nevertheless,

> "That blind clamor made me wise;"

"clamor" it was, the confused but persistent voice of inward feeling; "blind clamor," as not springing from or guided by intellect; nevertheless it "made" him "wise," saved him from the folly of denying God, at the bidding of the difficulties and doubts which the understanding will raise.

> "Then was I as a child that cries,
> But, crying, knows his father near."

These lines surely furnish a touching picture of man's present situation, assured indeed of God, but confronted by difficulties insurmountable by the cold reason.

"And what I am," originally written "what I seem," "beheld again what *is*," that is, God, real being, as distinguished from phenomenal existence, "and no man understands," the incomprehensible One; "and out of darkness," in which He is shrouded, "came the hands that reach through nature, moulding men." We see His working, we see not Him.

CXXV.

HOPE AND LOVE NOT WANTING EVEN WHEN THE MOST REGRETFUL LAYS WERE SUNG.

This poem, which is happily named by Genung the ministry of Poesy, is extremely important as shewing us the light in which we are to regard some of the darker and more despairing lyrics of In Memoriam. The Poet will have us know, that the doubts expressed in these were not always his own, that in the darkest hour hope was not extinct,

> "She did but look through dimmer eyes;"

" In his deepest self the Poet has never lost hope,"

> " Or love, but play'd with gracious lies,"

only played with them, did not really entertain them, and "play'd with them, because he felt so fixt in truth." Whether the strain were sad, or sweet and strong, love inspired it, love in the first place to his friend, a love which is to abide with him till death shall re-unite them,

> " . . . till I sail
> To seek thee on the mystic deeps,
> And this electric force, that keeps
> A thousand pulses dancing, fail."

CXXVI.

Love is King.

This brief poem is at once beautiful and difficult of interpretation; difficult, that is, when we endeavor to give definiteness to the thought involved. Mrs. Chapman, who so often expresses accurately and gracefully the main

CANTO CXXVI.

purport of the lyrics, seems at fault here. Her reading of the poem is " Love is and was his Lord and King—no finite sovereign—but that benign unfathomable Power to whom he consecrates his Elegy." These words, if we are not mistaken, misinterpret both the poem before us and the Prologue. The reference in the Prologue, as has been already seen, is to no mere impersonal " Power," however benign and unfathomable, but to the personal Christ, in whom perfect love is embodied. And the main, if not the exclusive reference of the Poet here, is to the love which has its seat in his own breast, and has for its object, the friend whose high qualities had been idealized by death. If this love has, perhaps, also to be viewed as typical of that love which he has come to recognize as the controlling power in the universe, evidently this cannot be regarded as anything but a subordinate thought in the poem. Genung seems to give its force correctly. His words are, " What has all along been cherished as a spirit within, to guide and bless and interpret, is now recognized as the masterpower of the life."

Love, in the first place for his friend idealized by death, but widening out to embrace others as well, has been his inspiration and solace. If light has come to him on the dark problems which death raises, it has been shed by or imparted to love; if faith in the great spiritual verities has been maintained, it has been due to love; if there has been force and sweetness in his song, it is because love breathed its spirit.

> "Love is and was my lord and king,
> And will be."

The fellowship with his friend is maintained through love. All messages from him came through or to love, and there are messages of wider import. He hears

> ". . at times a sentinel
> Who moves about from place to place,
> And whispers to the worlds of space.
> In the deep night, that all is well."

CXXVII.

"All is well."

This poem begins, where the former closed, taking up its last words, and explaining and qualifying them. "All is well," not for him alone and his friend, but for the world, which under the guidance of Him who is love, immortal love, is moving on amid convulsion and storms to a peaceful and happy issue.

> " All is well, though faith and form
> Be sunder'd in the night of fear ; "

The " form " of faith, as we have already seen, is those definite doctrinal propositions in which men's conceptions of God, and the spiritual verities generally, had come to be expressed. The Poet contemplates the loss of these, as taking place in the case of many " in the night of fear " or doubt, and yet the faith itself in its substance as retained by them. Thus far, therefore, " all is well," however appearances might seem to belie it.

The Poet anticipates, too, great and violent changes in society, fierce revolutions in which all that is most stable shall be upturned, and in the accomplishment of which the extremes of society, the very rich and the very poor, shall especially suffer. These impending changes are described in language, highly figurative and of great force,

> " The brute earth lightens to the sky,
> And the great Æon sinks in blood,
> And compass'd by the fires of hell ; "

The reference in the last line may perhaps be to the violent passions as well as to the dreadful sufferings of the time foreseen.

But " to those that hear, a deeper voice across

the storm" proclaims the spread of truth and justice; truth and justice between man and man. " Things that are made "—the institutions of human device and workmanship—" are shaken, that those things which cannot be shaken may remain." And he, his friend, looking with the light of the higher world in his eye, and *knowing* therefore, not simply believing in, but knowing, the goal of good to which all is tending, smiles at the convulsions and conflicts by which that goal is being reached.

CXXVIII.

"THE STRUGGLE AND VICTORY OF LOVE WITH DOUBT HAVE GIVEN AN INSIGHT INTO THE COURSE OF HUMAN THINGS AND TAUGHT TRUST IN THE FINAL ISSUE."—F.W.R.

The love which grappled with Death and overcame him; which not only defied death to quench it, but which in its quenchless vigor helped the Poet to maintain his faith in God and the Hereafter, spite of death's ravages—this love out of which faith in God and the Hereafter is in a manner born—has as its "comrade" "the lesser faith," that, namely, "which is concerned with the course of human affairs, as distinguished from the eternal realities." This "lesser faith" thus accompanied is "not overborne by present confusions," is not upset by the degradation and the disappearance of imperial races, such as those of Greece and Rome; "no doubt vast eddies in the flood;" it holds on to the hope of a happy consummation notwithstanding. And what it expects is not repetitions of the past in altered forms; if this were all which "the wild hours" bring, as it sometimes appears to be,

> " To draw, to sheathe a useless sword,"

useless, viz., on the supposition that no real progress was being reached,

> " To fool the crowd with glorious lies,"

lies, that is, which feed the crowd's love of glory, or,
> " To make old bareness picturesque
> And tuft with grass a feudal tower;"

a fine figure to set forth the mere external adornment of institutions or of usages, the essential injustice of which remains unchanged,—if this were all—then his scorn might well fall on these "wild hours." But what it expects is real progress towards a goal of ultimate good.

Nay, with eyes made wise by love, the Poet sees in part, sees dimly

> " That all, as in some piece of art,
> Is toil cöoperant to an end."

CXXIX.

HIS FRIEND MINGLES WITH ALL HIS EXPECTATIONS OF COMING GOOD.

In this poem the departed friend is addressed in terms of the most tender and reverent affection ; terms which find their only explanation in the fact that he has become idealized to the imagination of the poet by death. He is the same, and yet he is changed. His noble traits of character are irradiated by the glory of immortality; while in the Poet's case, all trace of sorrow has vanished, and there remains only an intense, ennobling and undying affection.

The explanation of the widely contrasting expressions applied to the departed should not be difficult.

> " So far, so near, in woe and weal ; "

"so far," as having passed beyond sight into another scene of being; "so near," *i.e.*, to thought and feeling, while remote to sense ;

> " Known and unknown ; human, divine : "

"known," as still retaining the individuality which had become familiar in the earthly life; "unknown," since the individuality has been inconceivably transfigured; "human" as ever, retaining all the human feelings; "divine," as "mixt with God" (cxxx.), in his thought;

"Loved deeplier, darklier understood;"

"loved deeplier," more intensely loved, since removed from sight: "darklier understood," less fully comprehended, since eternity has claimed him;

"O loved the most, when most I feel
There is a lower and a higher;"

that is, the object of most ardent affection to the Poet, when he is most alive to the great moral distinctions which obtain. It must ever be so, when the love is really moral.

"Behold, I dream a dream of good,
And mingle all the world with thee."

It is of the very nature of true and ardent love, one of its most common workings, thus to carry the thought of its object, and all the more if that object has been removed out of life, into any hope or experience of good. There is, however, something more specific here. The good of which the Poet dreams for the world is moral good, the ascendency as we have seen, of truth and justice; the dream of it could accordingly all the more readily recall him, who was the type to the writer of all he would have man become.

All this is far short of what some of the interpreters of Tennyson, with what appear Pantheistic leanings, have found in this and the following poem. For example, Genung says: "The immortal friend, in whom Divine Love has assumed a mysterious personality, is addressed as the type from which the world's ideal may be interpreted." While Davidson, going still farther, says: "The Poet now addresses his friend as an omnipresent spirit." There is nothing in the poem to justify, certainly nothing to necessitate, such an interpretation.

CXXX.

HIS PRESENCE FELT EVERYWHERE IN NATURE.

This is a companion poem to the preceding one, reasserting and amplifying the truth with which that poem closed. Nature, as observed, everywhere recalls his friend. That friend is present to his thought, his fancy, but surely to his thought and fancy only, in "the rolling air," the running stream, the rising and the setting sun. Tainsh says: " The dear, dead friend has become to the imagination of him who on earth loves him one with Nature and with God, humanizing them, yet not losing his own personality, but in that personality tender and near as ever, rising to the divine, and pervading the universal. Seen in all things, felt at all moments, he makes all things and all moments dear and holy by his presence."

> "What art thou then? I cannot guess;
> But tho' I seem in star and flower
> To feel thee some diffusive power,
> I do not, therefore, love thee less."

These words, it must be admitted, have a very Pantheistic cast, but as the personality of his friend evidently remains unbroken, and is the object of a love as real, only vaster than before, the Pantheism cannot be more than seeming, the blending with God and Nature can only be in the fancy or imagination of the Poet. The last stanza corroborates this view:

> " Far off thou art, but ever nigh;
> I have thee still, and I rejoice;
> I prosper, circled with thy voice;
> I shall not lose thee, tho' I die."

CXXXI.

Faith in the spiritual and the divine, incapable of establishment by logical proof, is closely connected with a pure and well-ordered life.

In Memoriam ends with a prayer, or what seems such. The "living will" which is invoked, might very naturally be regarded as the will of the Eternal, the will of God. It is so taken by Mrs. Chapman, who says: "The Poet's prayer ascends to that Eternal Power, who is over all, and through all, and in us all, that we may be purified." Unfortunately for this view, the Poet himself in a note inserted in Dr. Gatty's book, gives as the meaning "free will in man." In this statement of his meaning, he was anticipated by Davidson, who says the prayer is addressed to that "heaven-descended" "living will," which is the essence of human personality, and which shall endure,

> "When all that seems shall suffer shock."

The Poet summoned this "living will" to "rise like a fountain" in "the spiritual rock," with obvious reference to I. Cor. 10: 4, "flow thro' our deeds and make them pure," so that with action and character purified, our cry may rise from these earthly scenes

> "To One that with us works, and trust,
>> With faith that comes of self-control,
>> The truths that never can be proved
>> Until we close with all we loved,
>> And all we flow from, soul in soul."

Obviously the time to which the two closing lines point, is that of death; death being viewed not as the absorption of all souls into God, a conception expressly repudiated in poem xlvii., but as the close union of all with one another in God, the union even with the living, from whom in death "we flow."

Till then, the highest attainment within

reach is to "trust the truths," which are meanwhile incapable of intellectual proof or verification. This trust, according to the view presented in this poem, is not one to be easily or indolently reached. It comes, if it come at all, by the living will expressing itself in pure deeds and exercising full self-control. The closing poem of the series, therefore, bears testimony to the intensely moral character of the faith, which emancipates the soul from doubt and fear, and carries with it the assurance of future bliss.

THE EPILOGUE OR EPITHALAMIUM.

This Epilogue is not, properly speaking, a part of In Memoriam. Its occasion, its subject, one may say, was the marriage of a younger sister of the Poet, Cecilia, about the year 1842, to Edmund Law Lushington, for some time Professor of Greek in the University of Glasgow. Tennyson himself says, "it was meant to be a kind of Divina Commedia, ending cheerfully." The friend, whom he has enshrined in his Poem, is not forgotten in this Epilogue. The regret for him is dead; the love for him has grown. The bride was one, whose opening beauty as a child he admired, His silent, speechless presence at the marriage is imagined. And he reappears in the end as the type of the better race for which the world waits. The last lines are in complete harmony with the thought which he has reached towards the close of the Poem, and up to its highest level in loftiness.

"That friend of mine, who lives in God,

That God, which ever lives and loves,
One God, one law, one element,
And one far-off divine event,
To which the whole creation moves.